Fodor's POCKET

dublin

D0716760

fourth edition

Excerpted from *Fodor's Ireland*

fodor's travel publications
new york · toronto · london · sydney · auckland
www.fodors.com

contents

maps

on the road with fodor's

THE MORE YOU KNOW BEFORE YOU GO, the better your trip will be. Dublin's most fascinating small museum (or its most enticing crafts shop or friendliest pub) could be just around the corner from your hotel, but if you don't know it's there, it might as well be on the other side of the globe. That's where this book comes in. It's a great step toward making sure your next trip lives up to your expectations. As you plan, check out the Web as well. Guidebooks have been helping smart travelers find the special places for years; the Web is one more tool. Whatever reference you consult, be savvy about what you read, and always consider the source. Images and language can be massaged to make places appear better than they are. And one traveler's quaint is another's grimy. Here at Fodor's, and at our on-line arm, Fodors.com, our focus is on providing you with information that's not only useful but accurate and on target. Every day Fodor's editors put enormous effort into getting things right, beginning with the search for the right contributors—people who have objective judgment, broad travel experience, and the writing ability to put their insights into words. There's no substitute for advice from a like-minded friend who has just come back from where you're going, but our writers, having seen all corners of Dublin, are the next best thing. They're the kind of people you'd poll for tips yourself if you knew them.

Muriel Bolger is a travel writer and a columnist with both *Ireland on Sunday* and *Food & Wine Magazine*; she updated Dublin dining. She contributes to several national newspapers and magazines and is the editor of *Irish Interiors* and *Irish Exteriors*.

Anto Howard, is a Northside Dublin native who studied at Trinity College before acquiring his U.S. green card. He lived in New York, where he worked as a travel writer, editor, and playwright, before returning to Ireland. Anto (short for Anthony) is also the author of *Fodor's Escape to Ireland*.

Don't Forget to Write

Your experiences—positive and negative—matter to us. If we have missed or misstated something, we want to hear about it. We follow up on all suggestions. Contact the Europe editor at editors@fodors.com or c/o Fodor's, 280 Park Avenue, New York, NY 10017. And have a fabulous trip!

Karen Cure

Karen Cure

Editorial Director

dublin

introducing dublin

IN HIS INIMITABLE, irresistible way, James Joyce immortalized Dublin in his *Ulysses*, *Dubliners*, and *A Portrait of the Artist as a Young Man*, filling his works with the people he knew, with their own words, and with not a few of his own. As it turns out, he became one of Dublin's most famous exiles. Disappointed with the city's provincial outlook and small-town manners, he departed in 1902, at the age of 20 (his famed peers Sean O'Casey and Samuel Beckett soon followed). If, however, Joyce was to return to his genteel hometown today and take an extended, quasi-Homeric odyssey through the city (as he does so famously in *Ulysses*), would he even recognize Dublin as his "Dear Dirty Dumpling, foostherfather of fingalls and dotthergills"?

What would he make of Temple Bar—the city's erstwhile down-at-heels neighborhood now crammed with chic restaurants and stylish hotels in its reborn state as Dublin's "Left Bank"? Or the River Liffey quays, whose makeover has them standing in for Hollywood backlots? (Not so long ago, he would have found Daniel Day-Lewis acting in Jim Sheridan's film *The Boxer* near the Ha'penny Bridge.) Or of the new Irishness, where every aspect of Celtic culture is red-hot: Frank McCourt's *Angela's Ashes* has dominated best-seller lists in the United States (the movie version was shot in the city and elsewhere around the country), as has its sequel, *'Tis*; *Riverdance*, the old Irish mass-jig, has gone global; and even patriot Michael Collins has become a movie icon. Plus, the returned Joyce would be stirred by the songs of U2, fired up by the films of Neil Jordan, and moved by the poems of Nobel laureate Seamus Heaney. In short, Irish is way in. As for

Ireland's capital, elegant shops and hotels, galleries, art-house cinemas, coffeehouses, and a stunning variety of restaurants are springing up on almost every street in Dublin, transforming the genteel capital that once suffocated Joyce into a city almost as cosmopolitan as the Paris to which he fled.

Forget the Vikings and the English. Fast-forward to the new Dublin, where the army of invaders landing at the intersection of O'Connell Street and Temple Lane are London lads on a wild bachelor night, Europeans in search of a chic weekend getaway, and representatives from the United States of the "FBI"—or foreign-born Irish. Thanks to "the Celtic Tiger"—the nickname given to the roaring Irish economy—this most intimate capital city in Western Europe has become a boomtown.

Happily, enough of the old Dublin remains to enchant. After all, it's the fundamentals—the Georgian elegance of Merrion Square, the Norman drama of Christ Church Cathedral, a foamy pint at an atmospheric pub—that still gratify. Fittingly, some of the more recent developments hark back to the earliest. Two multimedia shows in the downtown area remind us that Norsemen (various neighborhood names, such as Howth, Leixlip, and Dalkey, echo their historic presence) were responsible for the city's original boom. In ancient days, more than 1,500 years ago, Dublin had been little more than a crossroads—albeit a critical one—of four of the main thoroughfares that traversed the country. Then, it had two names: Baile Atha Cliath, meaning City of the Hurdles, which was bestowed by Celtic traders in the 2nd century AD and which you can still see on buses and billboards throughout the city, and Dubhlinn, or "dark pool" (the murkiness of the water was caused by peat), which is believed to have been where Dublin Castle now stands.

In 837, Norsemen from Scandinavia carried out the first invasion on Dublin, only to be followed by other waves of warriors staking their claim to the city—from the 12th-century Anglo-Normans to Oliver Cromwell in 1651. Not until the 18th century did Dublin reach a period of glory, when a golden age of enlightened patronage by wealthy nobles turned the city into one of Europe's most prepossessing capitals. Streets and squares, such as Merrion and Fitzwilliam squares, were constructed with neoclassic dignity and Palladian grace. If, today, Dublin is still redolent in parts of the elegance of the 18th century, it is due to the eminently refined Georgian style of art and architecture, which flowered in the city between 1714 and 1820 during the English reigns of the three Georges. To satisfy the taste for luxury of the often-titled, unusually wealthy members of society, lemon-color chintz borders, gilded Derbyshire pier tables, and Adamesque wood paneling were installed in the salons of town houses. The arts also flourished: Handel, the German-born English composer, wrote much of his great oratorio *Messiah* here, where it was first performed in 1742. But the aura of "the glorious eighteenth" was short-lived; in 1800, the Act of Union brought Ireland and Britain together in a common United Kingdom, and political power moved from Dublin to London. Dublin quickly lost its cultural and social sparkle as many members of the nobility moved to the new power center, turning Ireland practically overnight into "the Cinderella of all nations," in historian Maurice Craig's words.

The 19th century proved to be a time of political turmoil and agitation, although Daniel O'Connell, the first Catholic lord mayor of Dublin (his statue dominates O'Connell Street), won early success with the introduction of Catholic emancipation in 1829. During the late 1840s, Dublin escaped the worst effects of the famine, caused by potato blight, that ravaged much of southern and western Ireland. As an emerging Victorian middle class introduced an element of genteel snobbery to the city, Dublin began a rapid outward expansion to the new suburban enclaves of Ballsbridge, Rathgar, and Rathmines on the southside and Clontarf and Drumcondra on the northside.

The city entered a period of cultural ferment in the first decade of the 20th century—an era that had its political apotheosis in the Easter Uprising of 1916. A war aimed at winning independence from Britain began in County Tipperary in 1919 and lasted for three years. During the Civil War, which followed the setting up of the Irish Free State in December 1921, the Four Courts and the Custom House both came under fire and were severely damaged. The capital had to be rebuilt during the 1920s. After the Civil War was over, Dublin entered a new era of political and cultural conservatism, which continued until the late 1970s. Amazingly, the major turning point in Dublin's fortunes occurred in 1972, when Ireland, emerging from 40 years of isolationism, joined the European Economic Community. In the 1980s, while the economy remained in the grasp of recession, Dublin and Ireland once again turned to the cultural sphere to announce themselves to the rest of the world. Irish musicians stormed the American and British barricades of rock and roll. Bob Geldof and the Boomtown Rats ("I Don't Like Mondays") and Chris de Burgh were among the most prominent of the musicians who found audiences well beyond their native shores, but it was U2, which climbed to the topmost heights of rock and roll stardom, that forged a permanent place in international popular culture for Irish musicians. Sinéad O'Connor, the Cranberries, and the Corrs have since followed, and more are on the fast track.

If the 1980s saw the ascent of Irish rock stars, the 1990s were truly the boom years—a decade of broadly improved economic fortunes, major capital investment, declining unemployment, and reversing patterns of immigration—all set in motion to a great extent by Ireland's participation in the EEC (now the European Union, or EU). When Ireland overwhelmingly approved the new EU treaty in 1992, it was one of the poorest European nations; it qualified for EU grants of all kinds. Since then, money has, quite simply, *poured* into Ireland—nowhere more so than in Dublin. The International Financial Services

Centre, gleaming behind the two-centuries-old Custom House, is one of the most overt signs of the success the city has had in attracting leading multinational corporations, particularly those in telecommunications, software, and service industries. In 2000 the government announced that Ireland was the world's biggest exporter of software. In the spring of 1998, the Irish overwhelmingly voted in favor of membership in the single European currency; since January 2002, Ireland's main currency has been the euro and the pound will be withdrawn from circulation.

Today, roughly half of the Irish Republic's population of 3.6 million people live in Dublin and its suburbs. It's a city of young people—astonishingly so. Students from all over Ireland attend Trinity College and the city's dozen other universities and colleges. On weekends, their counterparts from Paris, London, and Rome fly in, swelling the city's youthful contingent, crowding its pubs and clubs to overflowing. After graduating, more and more young people are sticking around rather than emigrating to New York or London, filling the raft of new jobs set up by multinational corporations and contributing to the hubbub that's evident everywhere.

All this development has not been without growing pains; with soaring house prices, increased crime, and major traffic problems, Dubliners are at last suffering the woes so familiar to city dwellers around the world. An influx of immigrants has caused resentment among some of the otherwise famously hospitable Irish. But you won't find many locals complaining, and progress steamrolls on. A new state-of-the-art Opera House and National Convention Center are both planned along the quays. "Me darlin' Dublin's dead and gone," so goes the old traditional ballad, but the rebirth, at times difficult and a little messy, has been a spectacular success.

In This Chapter

Updated by Anto Howard

here and there

IN DUBLIN'S FAIR CITY —"where the girls are so pretty" went the centuries-old ditty. Today, parts of the city—particularly the vast, uniform housing projects of the northern suburbs—may not be fair or pretty. But even if you're not conscious of it while you're in the city center, Dublin is in a beautiful setting: it loops around the edge of Dublin Bay and on a plain at the edge of the gorgeous, green Dublin and Wicklow mountains, rising softly just to the south. From the famous Four Courts building in the heart of town, the sight of the city, the bay, and the mountains will take your breath away. From the city's noted vantage points, such as the South Wall, which stretches far out into Dublin Bay, or from choice spots in the suburbs of south and north County Dublin, you can nearly get a full measure of the city. From north to south, Dublin stretches 16 km (10 mi). From its center, immediately adjacent to the port area and the River Liffey, the city spreads westward for an additional 10 km (6 mi); in total, it covers 28,000 acres. But its heart is far more compact than these numbers indicate. As in Paris, London, and Florence, and as in so many other cities throughout the world, a river runs right through Dublin. The River Liffey divides the capital into the "northside" and the "southside," as everyone calls the two principal center-city areas, and almost all the major sights in the area are well within an hour's walk of one another.

Coverage is organized into eight walks of the city center and the areas immediately surrounding it. The first two walks—The City Center : Around Trinity College and The Georgian Heart of Dublin—cover many of the southside's major sites: Trinity College, St. Stephen's Green, Merrion Square, and Grafton Street.

It makes sense to do these walks first, as they will quickly orient you to a good portion of the southside. The third walk—Temple Bar: Dublin's "Left Bank"—takes you through this revived neighborhood, which is the hottest, hippest zone in the capital. The fourth walk—Dublin West: From Dublin Castle to the Four Courts—picks up across the street from Temple Bar and gets you to the Guinness Brewery and Storehouse, the city's most popular attraction. The fifth walk—The Liberties—takes you on a brief stroll through working-class Dublin, a historic but often overlooked part of the city. Although the southside is split into five walks, you'll soon realize that the distance between the areas is not very great. The sixth walk—North of the Liffey—moves to the northside of the city center and covers all the major cultural sites there, including the James Joyce Cultural Centre, Gate Theatre, Dublin Writers Museum, and Hugh Lane Municipal Gallery of Modern Art. It also includes the rapidly developing Smithfield district, which locals are already hailing as the future "Temple Bar of the northside." The seventh walk—Along the Grand Canal—covers noteworthy sites along the canal, beginning in the northeast part of the city and ending in the southwest. Phoenix Park and Environs, at the western fringe of the northside city center, is the main focus of the eighth Dublin walk.

Because of its compact size and traffic congestion (brought on in the last few years by an astronomical increase in the number of new vehicles), *pedestrian* traffic—especially on the city center's busiest streets during commuting hours—is astonishing. Watch where you stop to consult your map or you're liable to be swept away by the ceaseless flow of the bustling crowds.

Numbers in the text correspond to numbers in the margin and on the Dublin City Center and Dublin West maps.

THE CITY CENTER: AROUND TRINITY COLLEGE

The River Liffey provides a useful aid to orientation, flowing as it does through the direct middle of Dublin. If you ask a native

Dubliner for directions—from under an umbrella, as it will probably be raining in the approved Irish manner—he or she will most likely reply in terms of "up" or "down," up meaning away from the river or down toward it. Until recently, Dublin's center of gravity was O'Connell Bridge, a diplomatic landmark in that it avoided locating the center to the north or south of the river, as strong local loyalties still prevailed among "northsiders" (who live to the north of the river) and "southsiders," and neither would ever accept that the city's center lay on the other's side of the river. But by the early 1990s, diplomacy had gone by the wayside. Now, Dublin's heart beats loudest southward across the Liffey, due, in part, to a large-scale refurbishment and pedestrianization of Grafton Street, which made this already upscale shopping address the street to shop, stop, and be seen. At the foot of Grafton Street is the city's most famous and recognizable landmark, Trinity College; at the top of it is Dublin's most popular strolling retreat, St. Stephen's Green, a 27-acre landscaped park replete with flowers, lakes, bridges, and—most of all—Dubliners enjoying a time-out.

A Good Walk

Start at **TRINITY COLLEGE** ①, exploring the quadrangle as you head to the Old Library to see the *Book of Kells*. If you want to see modern art, visit the collection housed in the Douglas Hyde Gallery of Modern Art, just inside the Nassau Street entrance to the college. If you're interested in the Georgian era, try to view the Provost's House and its salon, the grandest in Ireland. Trinity can easily eat up at least an hour or more. When you come back out the front gate, you can either stop in at the **BANK OF IRELAND** ②, a neoclassic masterpiece that was once the seat of the Irish Parliament, or make an immediate left and head up **GRAFTON STREET** ③, the pedestrian spine of the southside. The **DUBLIN TOURISM** ④ office is just off Grafton Street, on the corner of Suffolk Street. If Grafton Street's shops whet your appetite for more browsing and shopping, turn right down Wicklow Street, then left up South William Street to **POWERSCOURT TOWNHOUSE CENTRE** ⑤, where a faux-Georgian atrium (very dubiously set within one of Dublin's greatest 18th-century mansions) houses high-priced shops and pleasant cafés. The **DUBLIN CIVIC MUSEUM** ⑥ is next door to Powerscourt, across the alley on its south flank. If you're doing well on time and want to explore the shopping streets farther east, jog via the alley one block east to Drury Street, from which you can access the Victorian **GEORGE'S STREET ARCADE** ⑦. Whether or not you make this excursion, you should head back to Grafton Street, where **BEWLEY'S ORIENTAL CAFÉ** ⑧, a Dublin institution, is another good place for a break. Grafton Street ends at the northwest corner of **ST. STEPHEN'S GREEN** ⑨, Dublin's most popular public gardens; they absolutely require a stroll-through. **NEWMAN HOUSE** ⑩ is on the south side of the green. Amble back across the green, exiting onto the northeast corner, at which sits the grand **SHELBOURNE MÉRIDIEN HOTEL** ⑪, a wonderful place for afternoon tea or a quick pint at one of its two pubs. The **HUGUENOT CEMETERY** ⑫ is just down the street from the hotel, on the same side. If you want to see more art, make a detour to the **RHA GALLAGHER GALLERY** ⑬.

TIMING

Dublin's city center is so compact you could race through this walk in an hour, but in order to gain full advantage of what is on offer, it's best to set aside at least a half day—if you can—to explore the treasures of Trinity College and amble up and around Grafton Street to St. Stephen's Green.

Sights to See

❷ **BANK OF IRELAND.** Across the street from the west facade of **Trinity College** stands one of Dublin's most striking buildings, now the Bank of Ireland but formerly the original home of the Irish Parliament. The building was begun in 1729 by Sir Edward Lovett Pearce, who designed the central section; three other architects would ultimately be involved in its construction. A pedimented portico fronted by six massive Corinthian columns dominates its grand facade, which follows the curve of Westmoreland Street as it meets College Green, once a Viking meeting place and burial ground. Two years after the Parliament was abolished in 1800 under the Act of Union, which brought Ireland under the direct rule of Britain, the building was bought for €50,790 by the Bank of Ireland. Inside, stucco rosettes adorn the coffered ceiling in the pastel-hue, colonnaded, clerestoried **main banking hall,** at one time the Court of Requests, where citizens' petitions were heard. Just down the hall is the original **House of Lords,** with tapestries depicting the Battle of the Boyne and the Siege of Derry, an oak-paneled nave, and a 1,233-piece Waterford glass chandelier; ask a guard to show you in. Visitors are welcome during normal banking hours; a brief guided tour is given every Tuesday at 10:30, 11:30, and 1:45 by the Dublin historian and author Éamonn Mac Thomáis. Accessed via Foster Place South, the small alley on the bank's east flank, the **Bank of Ireland Arts Center** frequently exhibits contemporary Irish art and has a permanent exhibition devoted to "The Story of Banking." 2 *College Green, tel. 01/677–6801; 01/671–1488 arts center. €3.80. Mon.–Wed. and Fri. 10– 4, Thurs. 10–5; Arts Center Tues.–Fri. 10–4, Sat. 2–5, Sun. 10–1.*

⑧ BEWLEY'S ORIENTAL CAFÉ. The granddaddies of the capital's cafés, Bewley's has been serving coffee and buns to Dubliners since it was founded by Quakers in 1842 and now has four locations. Bewley's trademark stained-glass windows were designed by Harry Clarke (1889–1931), Ireland's most distinguished early 20th-century artist in this medium. The cafés make fine places in which to observe Dubliners of all ages and occupations; the aroma of coffee is irresistible, and the cafés' dark interiors—with marble-top tables, bentwood chairs, and mahogany trim—evoke a more leisurely Dublin. The food is overpriced and not particularly good, but people-watching here over a cup of coffee or tea is a quintessential Dublin experience. If you're interested in a more modern cup of coffee, check out

dublin city center

KEY

ℹ️ Tourist Information

SEE DUBLIN WEST MAP

ST. STEPHEN'S GREEN

N
0   330 yards
0   300 meters

Abbey Presbyterian Church, 56

The Ark, 27

Arthouse, 30

Bambrick's, 71

Bank of Ireland, 2

Bewley's Oriental Café, 8

Central Bank, 33

Custom House, 64

Dublin Civic Museum, 6

Dublin Tourism, 4

Dublin Writers Museum, 57

Gallery of Photography, 31

Garden of Remembrance, 59

Gate Theatre, 55

Genealogical Office, 22

General Post Office (GPO), 54

George's Street Arcade, 7

Government Buildings, 16

Grafton Street, 3

Ha'penny Bridge, 26

Hot Press Irish Music Hall of Fame, 52

Hugh Lane Municipal Gallery of Modern Art, 58

Huguenot Cemetery, 12

Irish Film Centre, 28

Irish Jewish Museum, 70

James Joyce Cultural Centre, 60

the Metro Café, nearby at 43 South William Street—it's one of Dublin's best haunts for the caffeine-addicted and its staff is devoid of the devil-may-care, pseudo-existential inefficiency that seems to plague so many other Dublin cafés. *78 Grafton St., tel. 01/677–6761 (for all locations); Sun.–Thurs. 7:30 AM–1 AM, Fri.–Sat. 7:30 AM–4 AM. 12 Westmoreland St.; Mon.–Sat. 7:30 AM–9 PM, Sun. 9:30 AM– 9 PM. 40 Mary St.; Mon.–Wed. and Fri.–Sat. 7 AM–6 PM, Thurs. 7 AM–9 PM.Jervis Shopping Centre, Jervis and Mary Sts.; Mon.–Wed. and Fri. 9 AM–6 PM, Thurs. 9 AM–9 PM, Sun. noon–6 PM.*

⑥ DUBLIN CIVIC MUSEUM. Built between 1765 and 1771 as an exhibition hall for the Society of Artists, this building later was used as the City Assembly House, precursor of City Hall. The museum's esoteric collection includes Stone Age flints, Viking coins, old maps and prints of the city, and the sculpted head of British admiral Horatio Nelson, which used to top Nelson's Pillar, next to the General Post Office on O'Connell Street; the column was toppled by an explosion in 1966 on the 50th anniversary of the Easter Uprising. The museum holds exhibitions relating to the city. *58 S. William St., tel. 01/679–4260. Free. Tues.–Sat. 10–6, Sun. 11–2.*

④ DUBLIN TOURISM. Churches are not just for prayers, as this deconsecrated medieval church proves. Resurrected as a visitor center, St. Andrew's, fallen into ruin after years of neglect, now houses Dublin Tourism, a private concern that offers the most complete information on Dublin's sights, restaurants, and hotels; you can even rent a car here. The office provides reservations facilities for all Dublin hotels, as well as guided tours, a plethora of brochures, and a gift shop (beware the exorbitant prices). Upstairs is a pleasant café serving sandwiches and drinks. *St. Andrew's Church, Suffolk St., tel. 01/605–7700 or 1850/230330 (within Ireland). www.visitdublin.com. July–Sept., Mon.–Sat. 8:30–6, Sun. 11– 5:30; Oct.–June, daily 9–6.*

⑦ GEORGE'S STREET ARCADE. This Victorian covered market fills the block between Drury Street to the west and South Great

George's Street to the east. It's changed little, despite a restoration. You'll find two dozen or so stalls selling books, prints, clothing (mostly secondhand), exotic foodstuffs, and trinkets. S. *Great George's St. Mon.–Sat. 9–6.*

★ ❸ **GRAFTON STREET.** It's no more than 200 yards long and about 20 ft wide, but brick-lined Grafton Street, open only to pedestrians, can make a claim to be the most humming street in the city, if not in all of Ireland. It is one of Dublin's vital spines: the most direct route between the front door of Trinity College and St. Stephen's Green, and the city's premier shopping street, home to Dublin's two most distinguished department stores, **Brown Thomas** and **Marks & Spencer.** Both on Grafton Street itself and in the smaller alleyways that radiate off it, there are also dozens of independent stores, a dozen or so colorful flower sellers, and some of Dublin's most popular watering holes. In summertime, buskers from all over the country and the world line both sides of the street, pouring out the sounds of drum, whistle, pipe, and string.

⑫ **HUGUENOT CEMETERY.** One of the last such burial grounds in Dublin, this cemetery was used in the late 17th century by French Protestants who had fled persecution in their native land. The cemetery gates are rarely open, but you can view the grounds from the street. It stands on the northeast corner across from the square. *27 St. Stephen's Green N.*

⑩ **NEWMAN HOUSE.** One of the greatest glories of Georgian Dublin, Newman House is actually two imposing town houses joined together. The earlier of the two, No. 85 St. Stephen's Green (1738), was designed by Richard Castle, favored architect of Dublin's rich and famous, and features a winged Palladian window on the Wicklow granite facade. Originally known as Clanwilliam House, it has two landmarks of Irish Georgian style: the Apollo Room, decorated with stuccowork depicting the sun god and his muses; and the magnificent Saloon, "the supreme example of Dublin Baroque," according to scholars Jacqueline O'Brien and Desmond Guinness, crowned with an exuberant ceiling aswirl with cupids and gods, created by the Brothers Lafranchini, the finest *stuccadores* (plasterworkers) of 18th-century Dublin. Next door at No. 86 (1765), the staircase is one of the city's most beautiful rococo examples, with floral swags and musical instruments picked out in cake-frosting white on pastel-color walls. Catholic University (described by James Joyce in *A Portrait of the Artist as a Young Man*) was established in this building in 1850, with Cardinal John Henry Newman as its first rector. At the back of Newman House lie **Iveagh Gardens,** a delightful hideaway with statues and sunken gardens that remains one of Dublin's best-kept secrets (you can enter via Earlsfort Terrace and Harcourt Street). The Commons Restaurant is in the basement. *85–86 St. Stephen's Green, tel. 01/475–7255. House and gardens €3.80. June–Aug. (guided tours only), Tues.–Fri. at noon, 2, 3, and 4; Sat. at 2, 3, and 4; Sun. at 11, noon, and 1.*

⑤ POWERSCOURT TOWNHOUSE CENTRE. Lucky man, this Viscount Powerscourt. In the mid-18th century, not only did he build Ireland's most spectacular country house, in Enniskerry, County Wicklow (which bears the family name), but he also decided to rival that structure's grandeur with one of Dublin's largest stone mansions. Staffed with 22 servants and built of granite from the viscount's own quarry in the Wicklow Hills, Powerscourt House was a major statement in the Palladian style designed by Robert Mack in 1774—a massive, Baroque-style edifice that towers over the little street it sits on (note the top story, framed by massive volutes, that was once intended as an observatory). The interior decoration runs from rococo salons by James McCullagh to Adamesque plasterwork by Michael Stapleton to—surprise—an imaginative shopping atrium, installed in and around the covered courtyard. The stores here include high-quality Irish crafts shops and numerous food stalls. The mall exit leads to the Carmelite **Church of St. Teresa's** and **Johnson's Court.** Beside the church, a pedestrian lane leads onto Grafton Street. *59 S. William St., tel. 01/679–4144. Mon.–Sat.*

⑬ RHA GALLAGHER GALLERY. The Royal Hibernian Academy, an old Dublin institution, is housed in a well-lit building, one of the largest exhibition spaces in the city. The gallery holds adventurous exhibitions of the best in contemporary art, both from Ireland and abroad. *15 Ely Pl., off St. Stephen's Green, tel. 01/661–2558. Free. Mon.–Wed. and Fri.–Sat. 11–5, Thurs. 11–8, Sun. 2–5.*

★ ⑪ SHELBOURNE MÉRIDIEN HOTEL. The ebullient, redbrick, white wood-trimmed facade of the Shelbourne has commanded "the best address in Dublin" from the north side of St. Stephen's Green since 1865. In 1921 the Irish Free State's constitution was drafted here in a first-floor suite. The most financially painless way to soak up the hotel's old-fashioned luxury and genteel excitement is to step past the entrance—note the statues of Nubian princesses and attendant slaves—for afternoon tea (€17.15 per person, including sandwiches and cakes) in the green-wallpapered **Lord Mayor's Lounge** or for a drink in one of its two bars, the **Shelbourne Bar** and the **Horseshoe Bar,** both of which are thronged with businesspeople and politicos after the workday ends. Elizabeth Bowen, famed novelist, wrote her novel *The Hotel* about this very place. *27 St. Stephen's Green, tel. 01/676–6471, www.shelbourne.ie.*

★ ⑨ ST. STEPHEN'S GREEN. Dubliners call it simply Stephen's Green, and green it is (year-round)—a verdant, 27-acre city-center square that was an open common used for the public punishment of criminals until 1664. After a long period of decline, it became a private park in 1814—the first time in its history that it was closed to the general public. Its fortunes changed again in 1880, when Sir Arthur Guinness, later Lord Ardilaun (a member of the Guinness brewery family), paid for it to be laid out anew. Flower gardens, formal lawns, a Victorian bandstand, and an ornamental lake that is home to many waterfowl are all within the park's borders, connected by paths. Strolling here or just passing through will offer up unexpected delights (be sure to look out for palm trees). Among the park's many statues are a memorial to Yeats and another to Joyce by Henry Moore, and the *Three Fates*, a dramatic group of bronze female figures watching over man's destiny. In the 18th century the walk on the north side of the green was referred to as the Beaux Walk because most of Dublin's gentlemen's clubs were in town houses here. Today it is dominated by the **Shelbourne Méridien Hotel.** On the south side is the alluring Georgian-gorgeous Newman House. *Free. Daily sunrise–sunset.*

★ ❶ **TRINITY COLLEGE.** Founded in 1592 by Queen Elizabeth I to "civilize" (Her Majesty's word) Dublin, Trinity is Ireland's oldest and most famous college. The memorably atmospheric campus is a must; here you can enjoy tracking the shadows of some of the more noted alumni, such as Jonathan Swift (1667–1745), Oscar Wilde (1854–1900), Bram Stoker (1847–1912), and Samuel Beckett (1906–89). Trinity College, Dublin (familiarly known as TCD) was founded on the site of the confiscated Priory of All Hallows. For centuries Trinity was the preserve of the Protestant church. A free education was offered to Catholics—provided that they accepted the Protestant faith. As a legacy of this condition, until 1966 Catholics who wished to study at Trinity had to obtain a dispensation from their bishop or face excommunication. Today more than 70% of Trinity's students are Catholics, an indication of how far away those days seem to today's generation.

Trinity's grounds cover 40 acres. Most of its buildings were constructed in the 18th and early 19th centuries. The extensive **West Front**, with a classical pedimented portico in the Corinthian style, faces College Green and is directly across from the **Bank of Ireland**; it was built between 1755 and 1759, possibly the work of Theodore Jacobsen, architect of London's Foundling Hospital. The design is repeated on the interior, so the view is the same both from outside the gates and from inside. On the lawn in front of the inner facade are **statues** of orator Edmund Burke (1729–97) and dramatist Oliver Goldsmith (1728–74), two other alumni. Like the West Front, **Parliament Square** (commonly known as Front Square), the cobblestoned quadrangle that lies just beyond this first patch of lawn, also dates from the 18th century. On the right side of the square is Sir William Chambers's **theater**, or **Examination Hall**, dating from the mid-1780s, which contains the college's most splendid Adamesque interior (designed by Michael Stapleton). The hall houses an impressive organ retrieved from an 18th-century Spanish ship and a gilded oak chandelier from the old House of Commons; concerts are sometimes held here. The **chapel**, which stands on the left of the quadrangle, has stucco ceilings and fine woodwork. Both the theater and the chapel were designed by Scotsman William Chambers in the late 18th century. The looming **Campanile**, or bell tower, is the symbolic heart of the college; erected in 1853, it dominates the center of the square. To the left of the campanile is the **Graduates Memorial Building**, or GMB. Built in 1892, the slightly Gothic building is now home to both the Philosophical and Historical Societies, Trinity's ancient and fiercely competitive debating groups. At the back of the square stands old redbrick **Rubrics**, looking rather ordinary and out of place among the gray granite and cobblestones. Rubrics, now used as rooms for students and faculty, dates from 1690, making it the oldest building still standing.

Ireland's largest collection of books and manuscripts is housed in **Trinity College Library**. Its principal treasure is the *Book of Kells,* generally considered the most striking manuscript ever produced in the Anglo-Saxon world and one of the greatest masterpieces of early Christian art. Once thought to be lost— the Vikings looted the book in 1007 for its jeweled cover but ultimately left the manuscript behind—the book is a splendidly illuminated version of the Gospels. In the 12th century, Guardius Cambensis declared that the book was made by an angel's hand in answer to a prayer of St. Bridget; in the 20th century, scholars decided instead that the book originated on the island of Iona in Scotland, where followers of St. Colomba lived until the island came under siege in the early to mid-9th century. They fled to

Kells, County Meath, bringing the book with them. The 680-page work was rebound in four volumes in 1953, two of which are usually displayed at a time, so you typically see no more than four original pages. (Some wags have taken to calling it the "Page of Kells.") However, such is the incredible workmanship of the *Book of Kells* that one folio contains the equivalent of many other manuscripts. On some pages, it has been determined that within a quarter inch, no fewer than 158 interlacements of a ribbon pattern of white lines on a black background can be discerned—little wonder some historians feel this book contains all the designs to be found in Celtic art. Note, too, the extraordinary colors, some of which were derived from shellfish, beetles' wings, and crushed pearls. The most famous page shows the "XPI" monogram (symbol of Christ), but if this page is not on display, you can still see a replica of it, and many of the other lavishly illustrated pages, in the adjacent exhibition—dedicated to the history, artistry, and conservation of the book—through which you must pass to see the originals.

Because of the fame and beauty of the *Book of Kells*, it is all too easy to overlook the other treasures in the library. They include the *Book of Armagh*, a 9th-century copy of the New Testament that also contains St. Patrick's Confession, and the legendary *Book of Durrow*, a 7th-century Gospel book from County Offaly. You may have to wait in line to enter the library; it's less busy early in the day.

The **Old Library,** aptly known as the Long Room, is one of Dublin's most staggering sights, at 213 ft long and 42 ft wide. It contains in its 21 alcoves approximately 200,000 of the 3 million volumes in Trinity's collection. Originally the room had a flat plaster ceiling, but in 1859–60 the need for more shelving resulted in a decision to raise the level of the roof and add the barrel-vaulted ceiling and the gallery bookcases. Since the 1801 Copyright Act, the college has received a copy of every book published in Britain and Ireland, and a great number of these publications must be stored in other parts of the campus and beyond. Of note are the carved Royal Arms of Queen Elizabeth I, above the library entrance—the only surviving relic of the original college buildings—and, lining the Long Room, a grand series of marble busts, of which the most famous is Roubiliac's portrait of Jonathan Swift. The Trinity College Library Shop sells books, clothing, jewelry, and postcards. *tel. 01/608–2308, www.tcd.ie. Long Room €5.70. June–Sept., Mon.–Sat. 9:30–5, Sun. 9:30–4:30; Oct.–May, Mon.–Sat. 9:30–5, Sun. noon–4:30.*

Trinity College's stark, modern Arts and Social Sciences Building, with an entrance on Nassau Street, houses the **Douglas Hyde Gallery of Modern Art,** which concentrates on contemporary art exhibitions and has its own bookstore. Also in the building, down some steps from the gallery, there's a snack bar with coffee, tea, sandwiches, and students willing to talk about life in the old college. *tel. 01/608–1116. Free. Mon.–Wed. and Fri. 11–6, Thurs. 11–7, Sat. 11–4:45.*

The **New Berkeley Library,** the main student library at Trinity, was built in 1967 and named after the philosopher and alumnus George Berkeley. The small open space in front of the library contains a spherical brass sculpture designed by Arnaldo Pomodoro. The library is not open to the general public. *College Green, tel. 01/677–2941. Grounds daily 8 AM–10 PM.*

In the Thomas Davis Theatre in the arts building, the **"Dublin Experience"** is a 45-minute audiovisual presentation devoted to the history of the city over the last 1,000 years. *tel. 01/608–1688. €3.80; in conjunction with Old Library, €7.60. Late-May–Oct., daily 10–5; shows every hr on the hr.*

THE GEORGIAN HEART OF DUBLIN

If there's one travel poster that signifies "Dublin" more than any other, it's the one that pictures 50 or so Georgian doorways—door after colorful door, all graced with lovely fanlights upheld by columns. A building boom began in Dublin in the early 18th century as the Protestant ascendancy constructed town houses for themselves and civic structures for their city in the style that came to be known as Georgian, for the four successive British Georges who ruled from 1714 through 1830. The Georgian architectural rage owed much to architects like James Gandon and Richard Castle. They and others were influenced by Andrea Palladio (1508–80), whose *Four Books of Architecture* were published in the 1720s in London and helped to precipitate the revival of his style, which swept through England and its colonies. Never again would Dublin be so "smart," so filled with decorum and style, nor its visitors' book so full of aristocratic names. Although Dublin's southside is a veritable shop window of the Georgian style, there are many other period sights to be found northside—for instance, the august interiors of the Dublin Writers Museum and Belvedere College, or James Gandon's great civic structures, the Custom House and the Four Courts, found quayside. These, and other Georgian goodies, are described in the Exploring sections of Dublin West and North of the Liffey.

A Good Walk

When Dublin was transformed into a Georgian metropolis, people came from all over to admire the new pillared and corniced city. Today, walking through Fitzwilliam Square or Merrion Street Upper, you can still admire vistas of calm Georgian splendor. Begin your Palladian promenade at the northeast corner of Stephen's Green—here, in front of the men's clubs, was the Beaux Walk, a favorite 18th-century gathering place for fashionable Dublin. Chances are you won't bump into a duke on his way to a Handel concert or an earl on his way to a rout, ball, and supper, but then, you won't have to dodge pigs either, which used to dot the cityscape back then. Walk down Merrion Street to **MERRION SQUARE** ⑭—one of Dublin's most attractive squares. The east side of Merrion Square and its continuation, Fitzwilliam Street, form what is known as "the Georgian mile," which, unlike some Irish miles, in fact measures less than a kilometer. On a fine day the Dublin Mountains are visible in the distance and the prospect has almost (thanks to the ugly, modern office block of the Electricity Supply Board) been preserved to give an impression of the spacious feel of 18th-century Dublin. Walk down the south side of the square to **NUMBER TWENTY-NINE** ⑮. Cut back through the square to visit the refurbished **GOVERNMENT BUILDINGS** ⑯, the **NATURAL HISTORY MUSEUM** ⑰, **LEINSTER HOUSE** ⑱, and/or the **NATIONAL GALLERY OF IRELAND** ⑲. The last leg of this walk is up Kildare Street to the **NATIONAL LIBRARY** ⑳, passing the back of Leinster House to the **NATIONAL MUSEUM** ㉑. Stop in at the **GENEALOGICAL OFFICE** ㉒ if you're doing research about your ancestors. Walk back to Stephen's Green and down Dawson Street, which runs parallel to Grafton Street. The **MANSION HOUSE** ㉓, **ROYAL IRISH ACADEMY** ㉔, and **ST. ANN'S CHURCH** ㉕ are on the left as you walk down toward Trinity College's side entrance.

TIMING

Dublin is so compact you could race through this walk in two hours, if you don't linger anywhere or set foot in one of the museums. But there are treasures galore at the National Gallery and the National Museum; the green tranquillity of Merrion Square; and many of Dublin's finest sites along the way (not to mention dozens of the city's most historic pubs)—so if you can, this is a good walk to do over the course of a half day.

Sights to See

㉒ **GENEALOGICAL OFFICE.** Are you a Fitzgibbon from Limerick, a Cullen from Waterford, or a McSweeney from Cork? This reference library is a good place to begin your ancestor-tracing efforts. If you're a total novice at genealogical research, you can meet with an advisor (€31.75 for an hour consultation) who can help get you started. It also houses the **Heraldic Museum,** where displays of flags, coins, stamps, silver, and family crests highlight the uses and development of heraldry in Ireland. Note that a map detailing the geographical origin of the hundred or so most common Irish surnames can be found at the back of this book (☞ Chapter 10). 2 Kildare St., tel. 01/603–0200, www.nli.ie. Free. Genealogical Office weekdays 10–4:30, Sat. 10–12:30; Heraldic Museum weekdays 10–8:30, Sat. 10–12:30. Guided tours by appointment.

16 GOVERNMENT BUILDINGS. The swan song of British architecture in the capital, this enormous complex was the last neoclassic edifice to be erected by the British government. A landmark of "Edwardian Baroque," it was designed by Sir Aston Webb—who did many of the similarly grand buildings in London's Piccadilly Circus—as the College of Science in the early 1900s. Following a major restoration in the early 1990s, these buildings became the offices of the Department of the taoiseach (the prime minister, pronounced tea-shuck) and the tánaiste (the deputy prime minister, pronounced tawn-ish-ta). Fine examples of contemporary Irish furniture and carpets now decorate the offices. A stained-glass window, known as "My Four Green Fields," was originally made by Evie Hone for the 1939 World's Fair in New York. It depicts the four ancient provinces of Ireland: Munster, Ulster, Leinster, and Connacht. The government offices are accessible only via 45-minute guided tours given on Saturday (tickets are available on the day of the tour from the National Gallery), though they are dramatically illuminated every night. Upper Merrion St., tel. 01/662–4888. Free. Sat. 10:30–3:30.

18 LEINSTER HOUSE. Built in 1745, Leinster House was commissioned by the Duke of Leinster and almost single-handedly helped to ignite the Georgian style that dominated Dublin for 100 years. It was not only the largest private residence in the city but the first structure in Ireland by Richard Castle, a follower of Palladio, who was to design some of the country's most important Palladian country houses. Inside, the grand salons were ornamented with coffered ceilings, Rembrandts, and Van Dycks, fitting settings for the parties often given by the duke's wife, Lady Emily Lennox, a celebrated beauty. The building has two facades: the one facing

Merrion Square is designed in the style of a country house; the other, on Kildare Street, is that of a town house. This latter facade—if you ignore the ground-floor level—was a major inspiration for Irishman James Hoban's designs for the White House in Washington, D.C. Built in hard Ardbracan limestone, the house's exterior makes a cold impression, and, in fact, the duke's heirs pronounced the house "melancholy" and fled. Today, the house is the seat of Dáil Éireann (the House of Representatives, pronounced dawl e-rin) and Seanad Éireann (the Senate, pronounced shanad e-rin), which together constitute the Irish Parliament. When the Dáil is not in session, tours can be arranged weekdays; when the Dáil is in session, tours are available only on Monday and Friday. The Dáil visitors' gallery is included in the tour, although it can be accessed on days when the Dáil is in session and tours are not available. To arrange a visit, contact the public relations office at the phone number provided. *Kildare St., tel. 01/ 618–3000, www.irlgov.ie.*

㉓ **MANSION HOUSE.** Home to the mayor of Dublin, the Mansion House dates from 1710, when it was built for Joshua Dawson, who later sold the property to the government on condition that "one loaf of double refined sugar of six pounds weight" be delivered to him every Christmas. In 1919 the Declaration of Irish Independence was adopted here. Dawson Street (named for the house's original tenant) is the site of the annual and popular **August Antiques Fair.** The house is not open to the public. *Dawson St.*

★ ⑭ **MERRION SQUARE.** Created between 1762 and 1764, this tranquil square a few blocks to the east of St. Stephen's Green is lined on three sides by some of Dublin's best-preserved Georgian town houses, many of which have brightly painted front doors above which sit intricate fanlights. Leinster House—Dublin's Versailles—along with the Natural History Museum and the National Gallery of Ireland line the west side of the square, but it is on the other sides that the Georgian terrace streetscape comes into its own, with the finest houses on the north border. Even when its flower gardens are not in bloom, the vibrant, mostly evergreen grounds, dotted with sculpture and threaded with meandering paths, are worth a walk-through. The square has been the home of several distinguished Dubliners, including Oscar Wilde's parents, Sir William and "Speranza" Wilde (No. 1); Irish national leader Daniel O'Connell (No. 58); and authors W. B. Yeats (Nos. 52 and 82) and Sheridan LeFanu (No. 70). Walk past the houses and read the plaques on the house facades, which identify the former inhabitants. Until 50 years ago, the square was a fashionable residential area, but today most of the houses are offices. At the south end of Merrion Square, on Upper Mount Street, stands **St. Stephen's Church** (Church of Ireland). Known locally as the "pepper canister" church because of its cupola, the structure was inspired in part by Wren's churches in London. *Daily sunrise–sunset.*

★ ⑲ **NATIONAL GALLERY OF IRELAND.** Caravaggio's *The Taking of Christ* (1602), Reynolds's *First Earl of Bellamont* (1773), Vermeer's *Lady Writing a Letter with Her Maid* (circa 1670) . . . you get the picture. The National Gallery of Ireland—the first in a series of major civic buildings on the west side of Merrion Square—is one of Europe's finest smaller art museums, with more than 3,000 works. Unlike Europe's largest art museums, which are almost guaranteed to induce Stendhal's syndrome, the National Gallery can be thoroughly covered in a morning or afternoon without inducing exhaustion. An 1854 Act of Parliament provided for the establishment of the museum, which was helped along by William Dargan (1799–1867), who was responsible for building much of Ireland's railway network in the 19th century (he is honored by a statue on the front lawn). The 1864 building was designed by Francis Fowke, who was also responsible for London's Victoria & Albert Museum.

A highlight of the museum is the major collection of paintings by Irish artists from the 17th through 20th centuries, including works by Roderic O'Conor (1860–1940), Sir William Orpen (1878–1931), William Leech (1881–1968), and Jack B. Yeats

(1871–1957), the brother of W. B. Yeats and by far the best-known Irish painter of the 20th century. Yeats painted portraits and landscapes in an abstract expressionist style not dissimilar from that of the later Bay Area Figurative painters of the 1950s and 1960s. His *The Liffey Swim* (1923) is particularly worth seeing for its Dublin subject matter (the annual swim is still held, usually on the first weekend in September).

The collection also claims exceptional paintings from the 17th-century French, Dutch, Italian, and Spanish schools. Among the highlights that you should strive to see are those mentioned above (the spectacular Caravaggio made headlines around the world when it was found hanging undiscovered in a Jesuit house not far from the museum) and Rembrandt's *Rest on the Flight into Egypt* (1647), Poussin's *The Holy Family* (1649) and *Lamentation over the Dead Christ* (ca. 1655–60), and, somewhat later than these, Goya's *Portrait of Doña Antonia Zárate* (circa 1810). Don't forget to check out the portrait of the First Earl of Bellamont, by Reynolds; the earl was among the first to introduce the Georgian fashion to Ireland, and this portrait stunningly flaunts the extraordinary style of the man himself. The French Impressionists are represented with paintings by Monet, Sisley, and Pissarro. The northern wing of the gallery houses the British collection and the Irish National Portrait collection, and the amply stocked **gift shop** is a good place to pick up books on Irish artists. Free guided tours are available on Saturday at 3 PM and on Sunday at 2, 3, and 4. *Merrion Sq. W, tel. 01/661–5133, www.nationalgallery.ie. Free. Mon.–Wed. and Fri.–Sat. 9:30–5:30, Thurs. 9:30–8:30, Sun. 12–5:30.*

⓴ NATIONAL LIBRARY. Ireland is one of the few countries in the world where one can happily admit to being a writer. And few countries as geographically diminutive as Ireland have garnered as many recipients of the Nobel Prize for Literature. Along with works by W. B. Yeats (1923), George Bernard Shaw (1925), Samuel Beckett (1969), and Seamus Heaney (1995), the National Library contains first editions of every major Irish writer, including books by Jonathan Swift, Oliver Goldsmith, and James Joyce (who used the library as the scene of the great literary debate in *Ulysses*). In addition, of course, almost every book ever published in Ireland is kept here, as well as an unequaled selection of old maps and an extensive collection of Irish newspapers and magazines—more than 5 million items in all. The main **Reading Room** opened in 1890 to house the collections of the Royal Dublin Society. Beneath its dramatic domed ceiling, countless authors have researched and written their books over the years. *Kildare St., tel. 01/661–8811, www.nli.ie. Free. Mon.–Wed. 10–9, Thurs.–Fri. 10–5, Sat. 10–1.*

★ ㉑ **NATIONAL MUSEUM.** On the other side of Leinster House from the National Library, Ireland's National Museum houses a fabled collection of Irish artifacts, dating from 7000 BC to the present. The museum is organized around a grand rotunda and elaborately decorated, with mosaic floors, marble columns, balustrades, and fancy ironwork. It has the largest collection of Celtic antiquities in the world, including an array of gold jewelry, carved stones, bronze tools, and weapons. The Treasury collection, including some of the museum's most renowned pieces, is open on a permanent basis. Among the priceless relics on display are the 8th-century **Ardagh Chalice,** a two-handle silver cup with gold filigree ornamentation; the bronze-coated, iron **St. Patrick's Bell,** the oldest surviving example (5th–8th centuries) of Irish metalwork; the 8th-century **Tara Brooch,** an intricately decorated piece made of white bronze, amber, and glass; and the 12th-century bejeweled oak **Cross of Cong,** covered with silver and bronze panels. The Road to Independence Room is devoted to the 1916 Easter Uprising and the War of Independence (1919–21); displays here include uniforms, weapons, banners, and a piece of the flag that flew over the General Post Office during Easter Week, 1916. Upstairs, Viking Age Ireland is a permanent exhibit on the Norsemen, featuring a full-size Viking skeleton, swords, leather works recovered in Dublin and surrounding areas, and a replica of a small Viking boat. In contrast to the ebullient late-Victorian architecture of the main museum building, the design of the **National Museum Annexe** is purely functional; it houses temporary shows of Irish antiquities. The 18th-century **Collins Barracks,** the most recent addition to the museum, houses a collection of glass, silver, furniture, and other decorative arts. *Kildare St.; Annexe: 7–9 Merrion Row; tel. 01/677–7444, www.museum.ie. Free. Tues.–Sat. 10–5, Sun. 2–5.*

⑰ **NATURAL HISTORY MUSEUM.** Dr. Stanley Livingstone inaugurated this museum when it opened in 1857. Today, it is little changed from Victorian times and remains a fascinating repository of mounted mammals, birds, and other flora and fauna. The Irish Room houses the most famous exhibits, skeletons of Ireland's extinct, prehistoric giant "Irish elk." The World Animals Collection includes a 65-ft whale skeleton suspended from the roof. Don't miss the very beautiful Blaschka Collection, finely detailed glass models of marine creatures, the zoological accuracy of which has never been achieved since. The museum is next door to the **Government Buildings.** *Merrion Sq. W, tel. 01/677–7444, www.museum.ie. Free. Tues.–Sat. 10–5, Sun. 2–5.*

⑮ **NUMBER TWENTY-NINE.** Everything in this carefully refurbished 1794 home, known simply as Number Twenty-Nine, is in keeping with the elegant lifestyle of the Dublin middle class between 1790 and 1820, the height of the Georgian period, when the house was owned by a wine merchant's widow. From the basement to the attic, in the kitchen, nursery, servant's quarters, and the formal living areas, the National Museum of Ireland has re-created the period's style with authentic furniture, paintings, carpets, curtains, paint, wallpapers, and even bellpulls. *29 Lower Fitzwilliam St., tel. 01/702–6165. €3.15. Tues.–Sat. 10–5, Sun. 2–5.*

㉔ **ROYAL IRISH ACADEMY.** Adjacent to the **Mansion House,** the country's leading learned society houses important manuscripts in its 18th-century library, including a large collection of ancient Irish manuscripts such as the 11th- to 12th-century *Book of the Dun Cow* and the library of the 18th-century poet Thomas Moore. *19 Dawson St., tel. 01/676–2570, www.ria.ie. Free. Weekdays 9:30–5.*

25 ST. ANN'S CHURCH (Church of Ireland). St. Ann's plain, neo-Romanesque granite exterior, erected in 1868, belies the church's rich Georgian interior, designed in 1720 by Isaac Wills. Among the highlights of the interior are polished-wood balconies, ornate plasterwork, and shelving in the chancel dating from 1723 and still in use for the distribution of bread to the poor of the parish. *Dawson St., tel. 01/676–7727, Free. Weekdays 10–4, Sun. for services.*

TEMPLE BAR: DUBLIN'S "LEFT BANK"

More than anywhere else in Dublin, it is Temple Bar that represents the dramatic changes (good and bad) and ascending fortunes of Dublin in the 1990s. Named after one of the streets of its central spine, the area was targeted for redevelopment in 1991–92 after a long period of neglect, having survived widely rumored plans to turn it into a massive bus depot and/or a giant parking lot. Temple Bar took off—*fast*—into Dublin's version of New York's SoHo, Paris's Bastille, London's Notting Hill: a thriving mix of high and alternative culture distinct from that in every other part of the city. Dotting the area's narrow cobblestone streets and pedestrian alleyways are new apartment buildings (inside they tend to be small and uninspired, with sky-high rents), vintage-clothing stores, postage-stamp–size boutiques selling €250 sunglasses and other expensive gewgaws, art galleries galore, a hotel resuscitated by U2, hip restaurants, pubs, clubs, European-style cafés, and a smattering of cultural venues. Visit the Temple Bar Web site (www.temple-bar.ie) for information about events in the area.

Temple Bar's regeneration was no doubt abetted by that one surefire real estate asset: location, location, location. The area is bordered by Dame Street to the south, the Liffey to the north, Fishamble Street to the west, and Westmoreland Street to the east. In fact, Temple Bar is so perfectly situated between everywhere else in Dublin that it's difficult to believe this neighborhood was once largely forsaken. It's now sometimes called the "playing ground of young Dublin," and for good reason: on weekend evenings and daily in the summer it teems with young people—not only from Dublin but from all over Europe—who fly into the city for the weekend, drawn by its pubs, clubs, and lively craic. It has become a favorite of young Englishmen on "stag" weekends, 48-hour bachelor parties heavy on drinking and debauching. Some who have witnessed Temple Bar's rapid gentrification and commercialization complain that it's losing its artistic soul—*Harper's Bazaar* said it was in danger of becoming "a sort of pseudoplace," like London's Covent Garden Piazza or Paris's Les Halles. Over the next few years the planned Smithfield development may replace Temple Bar at the cutting edge of Dublin culture, but for the moment there's no denying that this is one of the best places to get a handle on the city.

A Good Walk

Start at O'Connell Bridge and walk down Aston Quay, taking in the terrific view west down the River Liffey. Alleys and narrow roads to your left lead into Temple Bar, but hold off turning in until you get to **HA'PENNY BRIDGE** ㉖, a Liffey landmark. Turn right and walk through Merchant's Arch, the symbolic entry into Temple Bar (see if you can spot the surveillance cameras up on the walls), which leads you onto the area's long spine, named Temple Bar here but also called Fleet Street (to the east) and Essex Street (both east and west, to the west). You're right at Temple Bar Square, one of the two largest plazas in Temple Bar. Just up on the right are two of the area's leading art galleries, the Temple Bar Gallery (at Lower Fownes Street) and, another block up, the Original Print Gallery and Black Church Print Studio. Turn left onto Eustace Street. If you have children, you may want to go to the **ARK** ㉗, a children's cultural center. Across the street from the Ark, stop in at the Temple Bar Information Centre and pick up a handy *Temple Bar Guide*. Farther down Eustace Street is the **IRISH FILM CENTRE** ㉘, Temple Bar's leading cultural venue and a great place to catch classic or new indie films. In summer, the IFC organizes Saturday-night outdoor screenings on **MEETING HOUSE SQUARE** ㉙, behind the Ark, accessed via Curved Street. The street is dominated on one side by the **ARTHOUSE** ㉚ and on the other by the Temple Bar Music Centre. Dublin's leading photography gallery, the **GALLERY OF PHOTOGRAPHY** ㉛, is also here. Walk a few steps west to the narrow, cobbled Sycamore Street, and then turn right and walk to Dame Street, where you'll find the **OLYMPIA THEATRE** ㉜. Farther down Dame Street, the ultramodern **CENTRAL BANK** ㉝ rises above the city. Head for the corner of Parliament Street, where you can stop for a break or begin the next walk.

TIMING

You can easily breeze through Temple Bar in an hour or so, but if you've got the time, plan to spend a morning or afternoon here, drifting in and out of its dozens of stores and galleries, relaxing at a café over a cup of coffee or at a pub over a pint, maybe even watching a film if you're looking for a change from sightseeing.

Sights to See

㉗ **THE ARK.** If you're traveling with children and looking for something fun to do, be sure to stop by the Ark, Ireland's children's cultural center, housed in a former Presbyterian church. Its theater opens onto Meeting House Square for outdoor performances in summer. A gallery and workshop space host ongoing activities. *Eustace St., tel. 01/670–7788, www.ark.ie. Free. Weekdays 9:30–5:30, weekends only if there is a show.*

㉚ **ARTHOUSE.** This is one of the first purpose-built multimedia centers for the arts in the world. Its modern design—all glass, metal, and painted concrete—is the work of esteemed architect Shay Cleary Doyle, who intended the building to reflect the object glorified within: the computer. Inside are a training center, a performance venue, a creative studio, and an exhibition space that plays host to a variety of art exhibitions. Pride of place, however, goes to the Art Information Bureau and the Artifact artist's database, featuring the work of more than 1,000 modern Irish artists working in Ireland and abroad. This useful catalog is open to anyone wishing to buy or admire the work of the listed artists, and it is set up in such a way that you can search for work according to specific criteria; just press a few buttons and a list of artists and images of their work fitting your description will appear. An Internet café, Cyberia, is on the top floor. *Curved St., tel. 01/605–6800, www.arthouse.ie. Free. Weekdays 9–6.*

㉝ CENTRAL BANK. Designed by Sam Stephenson in 1978, the controversial, ultramodern glass-and-concrete building suspends huge concrete slabs around a central axis. Skateboarders and in-line skaters have taken up residence on the little plaza in front of the building. *Dame St., tel. 01/671–6666, www.centralbank.ie. Free. Weekdays 10–6.*

㉛ GALLERY OF PHOTOGRAPHY. Dublin's premier photography gallery has a permanent collection of early 20th-century Irish photography and also puts on monthly exhibits of contemporary Irish and international photographers. The bookstore is the best place in the city to browse for photography books and pick up arty postcards. *Meeting House Sq. S, tel. 01/671–4654, www.irish-photography.com. Free. Tues.–Sat. 11–6.*

㉖ HA'PENNY BRIDGE. This heavily trafficked footbridge crosses the Liffey at a prime spot: Temple Bar is on the south side, and the bridge provides the fastest route to the thriving Mary and Henry Street shopping areas to the north. Until early in the 20th century, a half-penny toll was charged to cross it. Yeats was one among many Dubliners who found this too high a price to pay—more a matter of principle than of finance—and so made the detour via O'Connell Bridge. Congestion on the Ha'penny has been relieved with the opening of the Millennium Footbridge a few hundred yards up the river.

28 IRISH FILM CENTRE (IFC). The opening of the IFC in a former Quaker meetinghouse in 1992 helped to launch the revitalization of Temple Bar. It has two comfortable art-house cinemas showing revivals and new independent films, the Irish Film Archive, a bookstore for cineastes, and a popular bar and café, all of which makes this one of the neighborhood's most vital cultural institutions and the place to be seen. *6 Eustace St., tel. 01/679–5744, www.fii.ie. Free. Weekdays 9:30–late, weekends 11–late.*

29 MEETING HOUSE SQUARE. Behind the Ark and accessed via Curved Street, Meeting House Square has become something of a gathering place for Dublin's youth and artists. Throughout the summer, seats are erected and a wide variety of events—including classic movies (every Saturday night), theater, games, and family programs—are held here. It's also a favorite site for the continuously changing street sculpture that pops up all over Temple Bar. All year round it's a great spot to sit and relax and engage in a bit of people-watching. It hosts an organic food market every Saturday morning. The square gets its name from a nearby Quaker meetinghouse.

★ **32 OLYMPIA THEATRE.** One of the best places anywhere in Europe to see live musical acts, the Olympia is Dublin's second oldest and one of its busiest theaters. Built in 1879, this classic Victorian music hall has a gorgeous red wrought-iron facade. Conveniently, two pubs are situated through doors directly off the back of the theater's orchestra section. The Olympia's long-standing Friday and Saturday series, "Midnight at the Olympia," has brought a wide array of musical performers to Dublin, and the theater has also seen many notable actors strut its stage, including Alec Guinness, Peggy Ashcroft, Noël Coward, and even Laurel and Hardy. In November 1996, when Van Morrison played Dublin, he chose to perform here rather than in a larger venue. If you have a chance to catch a favorite performer (or to discover someone new), come!—you won't regret it. *72 Dame St., tel. 01/677–7744.*

DUBLIN WEST: FROM DUBLIN CASTLE
TO THE FOUR COURTS

This section of Dublin takes you from the 10th-century crypt at Christ Church Cathedral—the city's oldest surviving structure—to the modern plant of the Guinness Brewery and its Storehouse museum. It also crosses the Liffey for a visit to Smithfield, the old market area being billed as the next hot location in the city. Dublin is so compact, however, that to separate out the following sites from those covered in the two other city-center southside walks is potentially to mislead by suggesting that this area is at some remove from the heart of the city center. In fact, this tour's starting point, City Hall, is just across the street from Thomas Read's, and Christ Church Cathedral is a very short walk farther west. However, the westernmost sites covered here—notably the Royal Hospital and Kilmainham Gaol—*are* at some distance, more so than may be comfortable if you're not an enthusiastic walker, so you may want to drive or catch a cab or a bus out to them.

A Good Walk

Begin with a brief visit to **CITY HALL** ㉞, and then walk up Cork Hill to the Castle Street entrance to **DUBLIN CASTLE** ㉟, whose highlights—the grand salons that show off Viceregal Dublin at its most splendid—are only visitable by a guided tour. The castle is also the new home of the **CHESTER BEATTY LIBRARY** ㊱, a world-renowned collection of Oriental art. Leave via the same gate, turn left, and walk up Castle Street to ancient **CHRIST CHURCH CATHEDRAL** ㊲, picturesquely situated on one of the few hills in the city. At the southeast corner of the cathedral, connected via an utterly beguiling Victorian-era bridge, **DUBLINIA** ㊳ gives you a chance to experience life in medieval Dublin. And just down Nicholas Street is—*begorrah!*—**ST. PATRICK'S CATHEDRAL** ㊴. If you're eager to venture back to the 17th century or love old books, visit the quaint **MARSH'S**

LIBRARY ㊵, next door to St. Patrick's. You can then stroll through the old artisan redbrick dwellings in the Liberties, home to the heaviest concentration of the city's antiques stores, to Thomas Street and—just follow your nose—the **GUINNESS BREWERY AND STOREHOUSE** ㊶, where you can keep your spirits up in more ways than one. At this point, if you want to see more architecture and modern art, proceed farther west to the Irish Museum of Modern Art in the elegant 18th-century **ROYAL HOSPITAL KILMAINHAM** ㊷, and the **KILMAINHAM GAOL** ㊸. If you don't elect to head this way, turn back down Thomas Street, crossing the Liffey at Bridge Street, which on its north side becomes Church Street. On your left is the **FOUR COURTS** ㊹. A little farther up on the left is **ST. MICHAN'S CHURCH** ㊺ and the beginning of the Smithfield area, which includes the **CEOL** ㊻, a museum dedicated to traditional Irish music. A quick jog over to Bow Street (via Mary's Lane) brings you to the **OLD JAMESON DISTILLERY** ㊼—here you'll learn all there is to learn about Irish whiskey. End your walk with a thrilling ride up the glass elevator to the top of the **CHIMNEY** ㊽.

TIMING

Allow yourself a few hours, especially if you want to include the Guinness Brewery and Storehouse and the Irish Museum of Modern Art at the Royal Hospital. Keep in mind that if you want to cover the easternmost sites—Dublin Castle, City Hall, Christ Church Cathedral, and environs—you can easily append them to a tour of Temple Bar.

Sights to See

★ � ㊻ **CEOL.** At the heart of the new Smithfield Village development is Chief O'Neill's complex, consisting of a hotel and Ceol, an interactive museum of Irish music. The museum tells the ancient story of Celtic music in a thoroughly modern fashion. The History of Irish Music area consists of five rooms dedicated to different periods from the age of myth and legend to the present. Computerized exhibits allow you to pick and choose as much detail as you want. The Stories Room contains a priceless oral history of musicians and storytellers from early in the 20th century. The Song Room illustrates the centuries-old Irish love of lyrics, from the haunting, unaccompanied *sean nós* style to the scatological Dublin ballad. The four major instruments of Irish music—fiddle, flute, button accordion, and *uilleann* (elbow) pipes (small, bellow-blown bagpipes played while sitting down)—are displayed on the ground floor. Throughout the museum, touch screens allow access to recordings of the masters of the genre plus hundreds of film clips of them performing. A children's area has an ingenious game of musical twister that allows kids to play along with a tune, using parts of their body to play the notes. *Smithfield Village, tel. 01/817–3820, www.ceol.ie. €6.35. Mon.–Sat. 10–6, Sun. noon–6.*

★ 36 **CHESTER BEATTY LIBRARY.** Formerly in the suburb of Ballsbridge, the library—one of Dublin's real hidden gems—is now housed in the gorgeous clock tower building of **Dublin Castle.** Sir Alfred Chester Beatty (1875–1968), a Canadian mining millionaire, assembled one of the most significant collections of Islamic and Far Eastern art in the Western world, which he then donated to Ireland. Among the library's exhibits are clay tablets from Babylon dating from 2700 BC, Japanese color wood-block prints, Chinese jade books, and Turkish and Persian paintings. The second floor is dedicated to the great religions and has 250 manuscripts of the Koran from throughout the Muslim world as well as one of the earliest gospels. Guided tours of the library are available on Tuesday and Saturday at 2:30 PM. On sunny days the garden is one of the most tranquil places in central Dublin. *Castle St., tel. 01/407–0750, www.cbl.ie. Free. Tues.–Fri. 10–5, Sat. 11–5, Sun. 1–5.*

✋ 48 **THE CHIMNEY.** Just in front of Ceol you'll see one of the original brick chimneys of the Old Jameson Distillery, which has been turned into into a 185-ft observation tower with the first 360-degree view of Dublin. Built in 1895, the redbrick chimney now has a two-tiered, glass-enclosed platform at the top. The ride up in the glass elevator is just as thrilling as the view. *Smithfield Village, tel. 01/817–3820, www.ceol.ie. €6.35. Mon.–Sat. 10–6, Sun. 11–7.*

37 CHRIST CHURCH CATHEDRAL. You'd never know from the outside that the first Christianized Danish king built a wooden church on this site in 1038; thanks to the extensive 19th-century renovation of its stonework and trim, the cathedral looks more Victorian than Anglo-Norman. Construction on the present Christ Church—the flagship of the Church of Ireland and one of two Protestant cathedrals in Dublin (the other is St. Patrick's just to the south)—was begun in 1172 by Strongbow, a Norman baron and conqueror of Dublin for the English crown, and went on for 50 years. By 1875 the cathedral had deteriorated badly, so a major renovation gave it much of the look it has today, including the addition of one of Dublin's most charming structures: a Bridge of Sighs–like affair that connects the cathedral to the old Synod Hall, which now holds the Viking extravaganza, Dublinia. Remains from the 12th-century building include the north wall of the nave, the west bay of the choir, and the fine stonework of the transepts, with their pointed arches and supporting columns. Strongbow himself is buried in the cathedral beneath an impressive effigy. The vast, sturdy **crypt,** with its 12th- and 13th-century vaults, is Dublin's oldest surviving structure and the building's most notable feature. At 6 PM on Wednesday and Thursday you can enjoy the glories of a choral evensong. *Christ Church Pl. and Winetavern St., tel. 01/677–8099, www.cccdub.ie. €2.55. Daily 9:45–5.*

34 CITY HALL. Facing the Liffey from Cork Hill at the top of Parliament Street, this grand Georgian municipal building (1769–79), once the Royal Exchange, was designed by Thomas Cooley and marks the southwestern corner of Temple Bar. Today it's the seat of the Dublin Corporation, the elected body that governs the city. Twelve columns encircle the domed central rotunda, which has a fine mosaic floor and 12 frescoes depicting Dublin legends and ancient Irish historical scenes. The building is home to an exhibition tracing the evolution of Ireland's 1,000-year-old capital. *Dame St., tel. 01/672–2204, www.dublincorp.ie. €3.80. Mon.–Sat 10–5:15, Sun. 2–5.*

35 DUBLIN CASTLE. Neil Jordan's film *Michael Collins* captured Dublin Castle's near indomitable status well: seat and symbol of the British rule of Ireland for seven and a half centuries, the castle figured largely in Ireland's turbulent history early in the 20th century. After extensive renovations, it's now used mostly for Irish and EU governmental purposes. The sprawling **Great Courtyard** is the reputed site of the Black Pool (Dubh Linn, pronounced *dove*-lin) from which Dublin got its name, though today it is lined with stretch limos and security guards. In the Lower Castle Yard, the **Record Tower,** the earliest of several towers on the site, is the largest remaining relic of the original Norman buildings, built by King John between 1208 and 1220. The clock tower building now houses the **Chester Beatty Library.** Guided tours are available around the principal **State Apartments** (on the southern side of the Upper Castle Yard), formerly the residence of the English viceroys. Now used by the president of Ireland to host visiting heads of state and EU ministers, they are lavishly furnished with rich Donegal carpets and illuminated by Waterford glass chandeliers. The largest and most impressive of these chambers, **St. Patrick's Hall,** with its gilt pillars and painted ceiling, is used for the inauguration of Irish presidents. The **Round Drawing Room,** in Bermingham Tower, dates from 1411 and was rebuilt in 1777; a number of Irish leaders were imprisoned in the tower from the 16th century to the early 20th century. The blue oval **Wedgwood Room** contains Chippendale chairs and a marble fireplace. The **Castle Vaults** now holds an elegant little patisserie and bistro.

On the grounds of the castle is the **Church of the Holy Trinity** (formerly called Chapel Royal), designed in 1814 by Francis Johnston, who also designed the original General Post Office building on O'Connell Street. Carved oak panels and stained glass depicting viceroys' coats of arms grace the interior. Look up to view the elaborate array of fan vaults that decorates the ceiling. On the outside more than 100 carved heads adorn the walls. St. Peter and Jonathan Swift preside over the north door, St. Patrick and Brian Boru over the east. One-hour guided tours of the castle are available every half hour, but the rooms are closed when in official use, so phone first. The easiest way in to the castle today is via the **Cork Hill Gate,** just west of City Hall. Castle St., tel. 01/677–7129, www.dublincastle.ie. State Apartments €4, including tour. Weekdays 10–5, weekends 2–5.

③⑧ DUBLINIA. In the old Synod Hall (formerly a meeting place for bishops of the Church of Ireland), attached via a covered stonework Victorian bridge to Christ Church Cathedral, Dublin's Medieval Trust has set up an entertaining and informative reconstruction of everyday life in medieval Dublin. The main exhibits use high-tech audiovisual and computer displays; there is also a scale model of what Dublin was like around 1500, a medieval maze, a life-size reconstruction based on the 13th-century dockside at Wood Quay, and a fine view from the tower. For a more modern take on the city, study the noted James Malton series of prints of 18th-century Dublin hanging on the walls of the coffee shop. St. Michael's Hill, tel. 01/679–4611, www.dublinia.ie. Exhibit €5. Apr.–Sept., daily 10–5; Oct.–Mar., Mon.–Sat. 11–4, Sun. 10–4:30.

④④ FOUR COURTS. Today the seat of the High Court of Justice of Ireland, the Four Courts are James Gandon's second Dublin masterpiece, built between 1786 and 1802, close on the heels of his **Custom House,** downstream on the same side of the River Liffey. The Four Courts replaced a 13th-century Dominican abbey that stood here earlier. In 1922, during the Irish Civil War, the Four Courts was almost totally destroyed by shelling, and the adjoining Public Records Office was gutted, with many of its priceless legal documents destroyed, including innumerable family records; efforts to restore the building to its original state spanned 10 years. Today the stately Corinthian portico and the circular central hall are well worth viewing. A distinctive copper-covered dome atop a colonnaded rotunda makes this one of Dublin's most instantly recognizable buildings; the view from the rotunda is terrific. Although there is no tour of the building, you are welcome to sit in while the courts are in session. Inns Quay, tel. 01/872–5555, www.courts.ie. Daily 10–1 and 2:15–4.

★ **41 GUINNESS BREWERY AND STOREHOUSE.** Founded by Arthur Guinness in 1759, Ireland's all-dominating brewer—in fact, at one stage the largest stout-producing brewery in the world—is on a 60-acre spread west of Christ Church Cathedral. It happens to be the most popular tourist destination in town—not surprisingly, since the Irish national drink is Guinness stout, a dark brew made with roasted malt. The brewery itself is closed to the public, but the **Guinness Storehouse** is a spectacular tourist attraction designed to woo you with the wonders of the "dark stuff." Located in a 1904, cast-iron–and–brick warehouse, the museum display covers six floors built around a huge central glass atrium. Beneath the glass floor of the lobby you'll see Arthur Guinness's original lease on the site, for a whopping 9,000 years. The exhibition shows all parts of the brewing process and its history, with antique presses and vats, a look at bottle and can designs through the ages, a history of the Guinness family, and an intriguing archive of Guinness advertisements. You might think it's all a bit much (it's only a drink, after all), and parts of the exhibit do feel a little over-the-top. But without doubt the star attraction is the top-floor **Gravity Bar,** with its 360-degree, floor-to-ceiling glass walls, which have a nonpareil view out over the city at sunset while you sip your free pint. One of the bar's first clients was one William Jefferson Clinton. *St. James' Gate, tel. 01/408–4800, www.guinness.com.* €11.45. *Apr.–Sept., Mon.–Sat. 9:30–7, Sun. 11–5; Oct.–Mar., daily 9:30–5.*

43 KILMAINHAM GAOL. Even farther west than the Royal Hospital, this is a grim, forbidding structure where leaders of the 1916 Easter Uprising, including Pádrig Pearse and James Connolly, were held before being executed in the prison yard. In the 19th century, other inmates here were the revolutionary Robert Emmet and Charles Stewart Parnell, a leading politician. You can visit the cells, a chilling sight, while the guided tour and a 30-minute audiovisual presentation relate a graphic account of Ireland's political history over the past 200 years from a Nationalist viewpoint. You can only visit the prison as part of a guided tour, which leaves every hour on the hour. There is also a small tearoom on the premises. *Inchicore Rd., tel. 01/453–5984, www.heritageireland.ie. €4.45. Tours Apr.–Sept., daily 9:30–5; Oct.–Mar., weekdays 9:30–4, Sun. 10–5.*

⑩ MARSH'S LIBRARY. A short walk west from St. Stephen's Green and accessed through a tiny but charming cottage garden lies a gem of old Dublin: the city's—and Ireland's—first public library, founded and endowed in 1701 by Narcissus Marsh, the Archbishop of Dublin, then open to "All Graduates and Gentlemen." The two-story brick Georgian building has been practically unchanged inside since it was built. It houses a priceless collection of 250 manuscripts and 25,000 16th- to 18th-century books. Many of these rare volumes are locked inside cages, as are the readers who wish to peruse them. The cages were to discourage students who, often impecunious, may have been tempted to make the books their own. The library has been restored with great attention to its original architectural detail, especially in the book stacks. *St. Patrick's Close off Patrick St., tel. 01/454–3511, www.kst.dit.ie/marsh. €2.55. Mon. and Wed.–Fri. 10–12:45 and 2–5, Sat. 10:30–12:45.*

⑰ OLD JAMESON DISTILLERY. Founded in 1791, this distillery produced one of Ireland's most famous whiskeys for nearly 200 years until 1966, when local distilleries merged to form Irish Distillers and moved to a purpose-built, ultramodern distillery in Middleton, County Cork. Part of the complex was converted into the group's head office, and the distillery itself was turned into a museum. You can watch a short audiovisual history of the industry, which actually had its origins 1,500 years ago in Middle Eastern perfume making, and tour the old distillery, where you can learn about the distilling of whiskey from grain to bottle. You can also view a reconstruction of a former warehouse, where the colorful nicknames of former barrel makers are recorded. There's a 20-minute audiovisual show, a 40-minute tour, and a complimentary tasting (remember: Irish whiskey is best drunk without a mixer—try it straight or with water); four attendees are invited to taste different brands of Irish whiskey and compare them against bourbon and Scotch. If you have a large group and everyone wants to do this, phone in advance to arrange it. *Bow St., tel. 01/807–2355, www.irish-whiskey-trail.com. €6.30. Daily 9:30– 5:30; tours every ½ hr.*

PHOENIX PARK – Europe's largest public park, a 20-or-so-minute walk west from the city center, extends about 5 km (3 mi) along the Liffey's north bank and encompasses 1,752 acres of verdant green lawns, woods, lakes, and playing fields. It's a jogger's paradise, but Sunday is the best time for everyone to visit: games of cricket, soccer, polo, baseball, hurling—a combination of lacrosse, baseball, and field hockey—and Irish football are likely to be in progress. Old-fashioned gas lamps line both sides of Chesterfield Avenue, the main road that bisects the park for 4 km (2½ mi). To the right as you enter the park, the People's Garden is a colorful flower garden designed in 1864. Among the park's major monuments are the Phoenix Column, erected by Lord Chesterfield in 1747, and the 198-ft obelisk, built in 1817 to commemorate the Duke of Wellington, the Irish general who defeated Napoléon for the British. You're guaranteed to see wildlife at the Dublin Zoo, the third-oldest public zoo in the world, founded in 1830, and just a short walk beyond the People's Garden. Both the president of Ireland and the U.S. ambassador have official residences in the park (the president's is known as Aras an Uachtarain), but neither building is open to the public. *tel. 01/677–0095 visitor center, www.heritageireland.ie.*

★ ㊷ **ROYAL HOSPITAL KILMAINHAM.** A short ride by taxi or bus from the city center, this replica of Les Invalides in Paris is regarded as the most important 17th-century building in Ireland. Commissioned as a hospice for disabled and veteran soldiers by James Butler, the Duke of Ormonde and Viceroy to King Charles II, it was completed in 1684, making it the first classical building in the city and a precursor of Dublin's golden age. It survived into the 1920s as a hospital, but after the founding of the Irish Free State in 1922, the building fell into disrepair. Over the last 15 years or so, restoration has returned the entire edifice to what it once was.

The structure consists of four galleries around a courtyard and includes a grand dining hall, 100 ft long by 50 ft wide. The architectural highlight is the hospital's Baroque **chapel,** distinguished by its extraordinary plasterwork ceiling and fine wood carvings. "There is nothing in Ireland from the 17th century that can come near this masterpiece," raves cultural historian John FitzMaurice Mills. Today the Royal Hospital houses the **Irish Museum of Modern Art.** The museum displays works by non-Irish, 20th-century greats like Picasso and Miró but concentrates on the work of Irish artists. Richard Gorman, Dorothy Cross, Sean Scully, Matt Mullican, Louis Le Brocquy, and James Colman are among the contemporary Irish artists represented. The Café Musée has soups, sandwiches, and other light fare. *Kilmainham La., tel. 01/612–9900, www.modernart.ie. Royal Hospital free; individual shows may have separate charges; Museum of Modern Art permanent collection free, small charge for special exhibitions. Royal Hospital Tues.–Sat. 10–5:30, Sun. noon– 5:30, tours every ½ hr; Museum of Modern Art Tues.–Sat. 10–5:30, Sun. noon–5:30; tours Wed. and Fri. at 2:30, Sat. at 11:30.*

⑮ ST. MICHAN'S CHURCH. Built in 1685 on the site of an older, 11th-century Danish church (Michan is a Danish saint), this Anglican church is architecturally undistinguished except for its 120-ft-high bell tower. But its 18th-century organ was supposedly played by Handel for his first-ever performance of the *Messiah,* and its Stool of Repentance is the only one still in existence in the city; parishioners who were judged to be "open and notoriously naughty livers" used it to do public penance. St. Michan's main claim to notoriety, however, is down in the vaults, where the totally dry atmosphere has preserved a number of corpses in a remarkable state of mummification. They lie in open caskets. Most of the preserved bodies are thought to have been Dublin tradespeople, although one is supposedly that of a religious crusader. *Lower Church St., tel. 01/872–4154. €2.55. Apr.–Oct.,*

weekdays 10–12:45 *and* 2–4:45, Sat. 10–12:45, Sun. *service at* 10 AM;
Nov.–Mar., weekdays 12:30–3:30, Sat. 10–12:45, Sun. *service at* 10 AM.

③⑨ ST. PATRICK'S CATHEDRAL. The largest cathedral in Dublin and
also the national cathedral of the Church of Ireland, St. Patrick's
is the second of the capital's two Protestant cathedrals (the other
is Christ Church). The reason that Dublin has two cathedrals is
that St. Patrick's originally stood outside the walls of Dublin,
and its close neighbor was within the walls and belonged to the
see of Dublin. Legend has it that St. Patrick baptized many
converts at a well on the site of the cathedral in the 5th century.
The original building, dedicated in 1192 and early English Gothic
in style, was an unsuccessful attempt to assert supremacy over
Christ Church Cathedral. At 305 ft, it is the longest church in the
country, a fact that Oliver Cromwell's troops—no friends to the
Irish—found useful as they made the church's nave into their stable
in the 17th century. Their visit left the building in a ruinous state,
and its current good repair is largely due to the benevolence of
Sir Benjamin Guinness, of the brewing family, who started to
finance major restoration work in 1860. Be sure to view the
gloriously heraldic **Choir of St. Patrick's,** hung with colorful
medieval banners, as well as find the tomb of the most famous
of St. Patrick's many illustrious deans, Jonathan Swift, immortal
author of *Gulliver's Travels,* who held office from 1713 to 1745.
Swift's tomb is in the south aisle, not far from that of his beloved
"Stella," Mrs. Esther Johnson. Swift's epitaph is inscribed over the
robing-room door. Yeats—who translated it thus: "Swift has
sailed into his rest; Savage indignation there cannot lacerate his
breast"—declared it the greatest epitaph of all time. Other
memorials include the 17th-century **Boyle Monument,** with its
numerous painted figures of family members, and the **monument
to Turlough O'Carolan,** the last of the Irish bards and one of the
country's finest harp players. To the immediate north of the
cathedral is a small park, with statues of many of Dublin's literary
figures and **St. Patrick's Well.** "Living Stones" is the cathedral's
permanent exhibition celebrating St. Patrick's place in the life of

the city. Matins (9:45 AM) and evensong (5:35 PM) are still sung on most days, a real treat for the music lover. *Patrick St., tel. 01/ 453–9472, www.stpatrickscathedral.ie. €3.45. May and Sept.–Oct., weekdays 9–6, Sat. 9–5, Sun. 10–11 and 12:45–3; June–Aug., weekdays 9–6, Sat. 9–4, Sun. 9:30–3 and 4:15–5:15; Nov.–Apr., weekdays 9–6, Sat. 9–4, Sun. 10–11 and 12:45–3.*

THE LIBERTIES

A stroll through the Liberties is a walk through working-class Dublin, past and present, good and bad. The name derives from Dublin of the Middle Ages, when the area south and west of Christ Church Cathedral was outside the city walls and free from the jurisdiction of the city rulers. A certain amount of freedom, or "liberty," was enjoyed by those who settled here, and it often attracted people on the fringes of society, especially the poor.

A Good Walk

Start on Patrick Street, in the shadow of St. Patrick's Cathedral. Look down the street toward the Liffey and a glorious view of Christ Church. Take a right on Dean Street, where you'll find John Fallons pub. Take a right off Dean Street onto Francis Street and walk uphill. A number of quality antiques shops line both sides of the thoroughfare. Halfway up Francis Street, on the right, behind hefty wrought-iron gates, is one of Dublin's most-overlooked treasures, **ST. NICHOLAS OF MYRA'S CHURCH** ㊾. Continue up Francis Street and take the next right onto Thomas Davis Street (named after a famous patriot and revolutionary— the Liberties has long had a close association with Irish Nationalism). The street is full of classic, two-story redbrick houses. The area, once the heart of "Darlin' Dublin" and the holy source of its distinctive accent, is rapidly becoming yuppified. Back on Francis Street, in an old factory building with its chimney stack intact, is the bustling **IVEAGH MARKET HALL** ㊿. At the top of Francis Street turn left onto Thomas Street. Across the road, on your right side, stands the wonderfully detailed exterior of St. Augustine and St. John, with its grandiose spire dominating the area around. You'll notice churches all over the Liberties; the bishops thought it wise to build holy palaces in the poorest areas of the city as tall, shining beacons of comfort and hope. Farther up Thomas Street in another converted factory is the **NATIONAL COLLEGE OF ART AND DESIGN** ⑤.

TIMING
Unless you intend on doing some serious antiques shopping, this is a relatively quick stroll—perhaps two hours—as the Liberties is a compact area of small, winding streets.

Sights to See

⑤⓪ **IVEAGH MARKET HALL.** One of numerous buildings bestowed upon the city of Dublin by Lord Iveagh of the Guinness family, the cavernous, Victorian, redbrick-and-granite Iveagh Market Hall holds an eclectic market from Tuesday to Saturday. *Francis St. Free. Tues.–Sat. 9–5.*

⑤① **NATIONAL COLLEGE OF ART AND DESIGN.** The delicate welding of glass and iron onto the redbrick Victorian facade of this onetime factory makes this school worth a visit. Walk around the cobblestone central courtyard, where there's always the added bonus of viewing some of the students work in mediums such as glass, clay, metal, and stone. *Thomas St., tel. 01/671–1377, www.ncad.ie. Free. Weekdays 9–7.*

④⑨ **ST. NICHOLAS OF MYRA'S CHURCH.** This church was completed in 1834 in grand neoclassic style. Inside, the highly ornate chapel includes ceiling panels of each of the Twelve Apostles and a pietà raised 20 ft above the marble altar, which is guarded on each side by angels sculpted by John Hogan while he was in Florence. The tiny nuptial chapel to the right has a small Harry Clarke stained-glass window. *St. Nicholas St. Free. Hrs vary.*

NORTH OF THE LIFFEY

If you stand on O'Connell Bridge or the pedestrian-only Ha'penny span, you'll get excellent views up and down the Liffey, the *abha na life*, which James Joyce transcribed phonetically as Anna Livia in *Finnegan's Wake*. Here, framed with embankments just like those along Paris's Seine, the river is near the end of its 128-km (80-mi) journey from the Wicklow Mountains to the Irish Sea. And near here, you begin a pilgrimage into James Joyce Country and the fascinating sights of Dublin's northside.

Today the northside—a mix of densely thronged shopping streets and run-down sections (though the property boom is rapidly refurbishing these areas) of once-genteel homes— absolutely warrants a walk for three reasons: its major cultural institutions (which include the Gate Theatre, the James Joyce Cultural Centre, the Dublin Writers Museum, and the Hugh Lane Municipal Gallery of Modern Art), the number of sites of significance with ties to Irish Republicanism, and its busy streets. During the 18th century, most of the upper echelons of Dublin society lived in the Georgian houses around Mountjoy Square and shopped along Capel Street, which was lined with stores stocking fine furniture and silver. The construction of Merrion Square on the southside (completed in 1764) and nearby Fitzwilliam Square (completed in 1825), and the decision by Ireland's grandest duke to build Leinster House on the southside, permanently changed the northside's fortunes. The city's fashionable social center crossed the Liffey, and although some of the northside's illustrious inhabitants clung to their houses, this area gradually became more run-down. The northside's fortunes may be changing, though. Once-derelict swaths of houses, especially on and near the Liffey, are being rehabilitated, and a large new shopping center opened on Mary Street in late 1996. Now a huge shopping mall and entertainment complex are planned for O'Connell Street, right where the defunct Carlton Cinema stands. Still, the redevelopment that has swept through Temple Bar is only in its early stages here, but perhaps because it's on the cusp of transition, it's an interesting part of town to visit.

A Good Walk

Begin at O'Connell Bridge—if you look closely at it you will notice that it is wider than it is long—and head north up **O'CONNELL STREET** ⑥. Stop to admire the monument to Daniel O'Connell, "The Liberator," erected as a tribute to the great orator's achievement in securing Catholic Emancipation in 1829 (note the obvious scars from the fighting of 1916 on the figures). A quick trip down middle Abbey Street takes you to the brand-new **HOT PRESS IRISH MUSIC HALL OF FAME** ⑫, a museum dedicated to Irish pop music. Then continue north to the **GENERAL POST OFFICE** ⑭, a major site in the Easter Uprising of 1916. O'Connell leads to the southeastern corner of Parnell Square. Heading counterclockwise around the square, you'll pass in turn the **GATE THEATRE** ⑮ and **ABBEY PRESBYTERIAN CHURCH** ⑯ before coming to the **DUBLIN WRITERS MUSEUM** ⑰ and the **HUGH LANE MUNICIPAL GALLERY OF MODERN ART** ⑱, both on the north side of the square and both housed in splendid neoclassic mansions; you should plan to spend most of your time at these two sites while on the northside. Either before you go in or after you come out, you might also want to visit the solemn yet serene **GARDEN OF REMEMBRANCE** ⑲.

From here, you have two choices: to continue exploring the cultural sights that lie to the northeast of Parnell Square and east of O'Connell Street or to head to Moore, Henry, and Mary streets for a flavor of middle-class Dublin that you won't get on the spiffier southside. If you decide to continue your cultural explorations, jump two blocks northeast of Parnell Square to the **JAMES JOYCE CULTURAL CENTRE** ⑳, and then head farther northeast to the once glamorous **MOUNTJOY SQUARE** ㉑. From here, turn south, stopping in at the **ST. FRANCIS XAVIER**

CHURCH ⑥ on Gardiner Street. Head back west to Marlborough Street (parallel to and between Gardiner and O'Connell streets) to visit the **PRO-CATHEDRAL** ⑥. Continue down to the quays and jog a block east to the **CUSTOM HOUSE** ⑥. Or if you decide to shop with the locals, leave Parnell Square via the southwestern corner, stopping first to check out the chapel at the **ROTUNDA HOSPITAL** ⑥; Moore Street is your first left off Parnell Street and leads directly to Henry Street.

TIMING
The northside has fewer major attractions than the southside and, overall, is less picturesque. As a result, you're unlikely to want to stroll as leisurely here. If you zip right through this walk, you could be done in less than two hours. But the two major cultural institutions covered here—the Dublin Writers Museum and the Hugh Lane Municipal Gallery of Modern Art—easily deserve several hours each, so it's worth doing this walk only if you have the time to devote to them.

Sights to See

⑤ **ABBEY PRESBYTERIAN CHURCH.** A soaring spire marks the exterior of this church, popularly known as Findlater's Church, after Alex Findlater, a noted Dublin grocer who endowed it. Completed in 1864, the church stands on the northeast corner of Parnell Square; the inside has a stark Presbyterian atmosphere, despite stained-glass windows and ornate pews. For a bird's-eye view, take the small staircase that leads to the balcony. *Parnell Sq., tel. 01/837–8600. Free. Hrs vary.*

⑥ **CUSTOM HOUSE.** Seen at its best reflected in the waters of the Liffey during the short interval when the high tide is on the turn, the Custom House is the city's most spectacular Georgian building. Extending 375 ft on the north side of the river, this is the work of James Gandon, an English architect who arrived in Ireland in 1781, when construction commenced (it continued for 10 years). Crafted from gleaming Portland stone, the central portico is linked by arcades to the pavilions at either end. Too bad the dome is on the puny side and out of proportion. A statue of Commerce tops the graceful copper dome; statues on the main facade are based on allegorical themes. Note the exquisitely carved lions and unicorns supporting the arms of Ireland at the far ends of the facade. Republicans set the building on fire in 1921, but it has been completely restored and now houses government offices. The building opened to the public in mid-1997 after having been closed for many years, and with it came a new visitor center tracing the building's history and significance, and the life of Gandon. *Custom House Quay, tel.* 01/878–7660. €1.27. *Mid-Mar.–Oct, weekdays* 10–5:30, *weekends* 2–5:30; *Nov.–Feb., Wed.–Fri.* 10–5, *Sun.* 2–5:30.

★ ⑤ **DUBLIN WRITERS MUSEUM.** "If you would know Ireland—body and soul—you must read its poems and stories," wrote Yeats in 1891. Further investigation into the Irish way with words can be found here at this unique museum, set within a magnificently restored 18th-century town house on the north side of Parnell Square. Once the home of John Jameson (of the Irish whiskey family), the mansion is centered around an enormous drawing room, gorgeously decorated with paintings, Adamesque plasterwork, and a deep Edwardian lincrusta frieze. Rare manuscripts, diaries, posters, letters, limited and first editions, photographs, and other mementoes commemorate the life and works of the nation's greatest writers (and there are *many* of them, so leave plenty of time), including Joyce, Shaw, J. M. Synge, Lady Gregory, Yeats, Beckett, and many others. On display are an 1804 edition of Swift's *Gulliver's Travels*, an 1899 first edition of Bram Stoker's *Dracula*, and an 1899 edition of Wilde's *Ballad of Reading Gaol*. There's even a special "Teller of Tales" exhibit showcasing Behan, O'Flaherty, and O'Faolan. Readings are periodically held. The bookshop and café make this an ideal place to spend a rainy afternoon. If you lose track of time and stay until the closing hour, you might want to dine at Chapter One, a highly regarded restaurant in the basement (☞ *Dining, below*), which would have had Joyce ecstasizing about its currant-sprinkled scones. 18 Parnell Sq. N, tel. 01/872–2077, www.visitdublin.com. €5.10. June–Aug., Mon.–Sat. 10–6, Sun. 11–5; Sept.–May, Mon.–Sat. 10–5, Sun. 11–5.

59 GARDEN OF REMEMBRANCE. Opened in 1966, 50 years after the Easter Uprising of 1916, the garden, within Parnell Square, commemorates all those who died fighting for Irish freedom. A large plaza is at the garden's entrance; steps lead down to the fountain area, graced with a sculpture by contemporary Irish artist Oisín Kelly based on the mythological Children of Lír, who were turned into swans. The garden serves as an oasis of tranquillity in the middle of the busy city. Parnell Sq. Daily 9–5.

55 GATE THEATRE. The Gate has been one of Dublin's most important theaters since its founding in 1929 by Micháel MacLiammóir and Hilton Edwards, who also founded Galway City's An Taibhdhearc as the national Irish-language theater. Many innovative productions by Irish playwrights have been staged here, and Dublin audiences have encountered foreign playwrights and actors here as well, including Orson Welles (his first paid performance) and James Mason, who also performed here early in his career. The show actually begins as soon as you walk into the auditorium—a Georgian masterwork designed by Richard Johnston in 1784 as an assembly room for the Rotunda Hospital complex. Today the theater plays it safe with a major repertory of European and North American drama and new plays by established Irish writers. Cavendish Row, tel. 01/874–4045. Shows Mon.–Sat.

54 GENERAL POST OFFICE. Known as the GPO, it is one of the great civic buildings of Dublin's Georgian era, but its fame derives from the role it played during the Easter Uprising. It has an impressive facade in the neoclassic style and was designed by Francis Johnston and built by the British between 1814 and 1818 as a center of communications. This gave it great strategic importance and was one of the reasons why it was chosen by the insurgent forces in 1916 as a headquarters. Here, on Easter Monday, 1916, the Republican forces, about 2,000 in number and under the guidance of Pádrig Pearse and James Connolly, stormed the building and issued the Proclamation of the Irish Republic. After a week of shelling, the GPO lay in ruins; 13 rebels were ultimately executed (including Connolly, who was dying of gangrene from a leg shattered in the fighting and had to be propped up in a chair before the firing squad). Most of the original building was destroyed, though the facade survived (you can still see the scars of bullets on its pillars). Rebuilt and subsequently reopened in 1929, it is still a working post office, with an attractive two-story main concourse. A bronze sculpture depicting the dying Cuchulainn, a leader of the Red Branch Knights in Celtic mythology, sits in the front window. The 1916 Proclamation and the names of its signatories are inscribed on the green marble plinth. *O'Connell St., tel. 01/872–8888, www.anpost.ie. Free. Mon.–Sat. 8–8, Sun. 10:30–6.*

52 **HOT PRESS IRISH MUSIC HALL OF FAME.** In 1999 Ireland's flagship music magazine had the clever idea to open a museum dedicated to Irish rock and pop music. Ireland has had a large impact on the world music scene, and the Hall of Fame is like a garage sale for the greats of Irish pop music: Van Morrison's big hat, Bob Geldof's cheap guitar, Sinéad O'Connor's self-mutilated jeans, the Corr's infinitesimally small dresses, and, of course, Bono's superfly Zooropa shoes—all neatly piled in chronological order. The self-guided audio tour takes you through the highs and lows of this musical journey, from the Beat bands of the '60s; '70s punk bands with rockin' names like Stiff Little Fingers; the 1980s, when U2 was the world's most popular band; through to the boy bands and diva-driven (Sinéad, Andrea Corr, Delores O'Riordian of the Cranberries) '90s scene. Favorite items include Sinéad O'Connor's first royalty check from Island records for £13.66. It's uncashed. *57 Middle Abbey St., tel. 01/878–3345, www.imhf.com. €5.70. Apr.–Sept., daily 10–6; Oct.–Mar., daily 11–5.*

★ 58 HUGH LANE MUNICIPAL GALLERY OF MODERN ART. Built originally as a town house for the Earl of Charlemont in 1762, this residence was so grand its Parnell Square street was nicknamed "Palace Row" in its honor. Designed by Sir William Chambers (who also built the Marino Casino for Charlemont) in the best Palladian manner, its delicate and rigidly correct facade, extended by two demilune arcades, was fashioned from the "new" white Ardmulcan stone (now seasoned to gray). Charlemont was one of the cultural locomotives of 18th-century Dublin—his walls were hung with Titians and Hogarths, and he frequently dined with Oliver Goldsmith and Sir Joshua Reynolds—so he would undoubtedly be delighted that his home is now the Hugh Lane Gallery, named after a nephew of Lady Gregory (Yeats's aristocratic patron). Lane collected both Impressionist paintings and 19th-century Irish and Anglo-Irish works. A complicated agreement with the National Gallery in London (reached after heated diplomatic dispute) stipulates that a portion of the 39 French paintings amassed by Lane shuttle back and forth between London and here. You can see Pissarro's *Printemps*, Manet's *Eva Gonzales*, Morisot's *Jour d'Été*, and, the jewel of the collection, Renoir's *Les Parapluies*.

In early 2000 the late Francis Bacon's partner donated the entire contents of the artist's studio to the Hugh Lane Gallery. In something of a snub to the British art establishment, the studio of arguably Britain's premier 20th-century artist will be reconstructed in all its gaudy glory in Dublin. Bacon is responsible for such works as *Study After Velázquez 1950* and the tragic splash-and-crash *Triptych*. The reconstructed studio will remain on permanent display, along with Bacon's diary (that should be worth a read), books, and anything else they picked up off his floor.

Between the collection of Irish paintings in the **National Gallery of Ireland** and the superlative works on view here, you can quickly become familiar with 20th-century Irish art. Irish artists represented include Roderic O'Conor, well known for his views of the West of Ireland; William Leech, including his *Girl with a Tinsel Scarf* (circa 1912) and *The Cigarette*; and the most famous of the group, Jack B. Yeats (W. B.'s brother). The museum has a dozen of his paintings, including *Ball Alley* (ca. 1927) and *There Is No Night* (1949). There is also strikingly displayed stained-glass work by early 20th-century Irish master artisans Harry Clarke and Evie Hone. *Parnell Sq. N, tel. 01/874–1903, www.hughlane.ie. Free. Tues.–Thurs. 9:30–6, Fri.–Sat. 9:30–5, Sun. 11–5.*

60 JAMES JOYCE CULTURAL CENTRE. Not everyone in Ireland has read James Joyce, but everyone has heard of him—especially since a copy of his censored and suppressed *Ulysses* was one of the top status symbols of the early 20th century. Today, of course, Joyce is acknowledged as one of the greatest modern authors, and his *Dubliners*, *Finnegan's Wake*, and *A Portrait of the Artist as a Young Man* can even be read as poetic "travel guides" to Dublin. Now open to the general public, this restored 18th-century Georgian town house, once the dancing academy of Professor Denis J. Maginni, is a center for Joycean studies and events related to the author. It has an extensive library and archives, exhibition rooms, a bookstore, and a café. Along with housing the **Joyce Museum** in Sandycove, the center is the main organizer of "Bloomstime," which marks the week leading up to June 16's Bloomsday celebrations. *35 N. Great George's St., tel. 01/878–8547, www.jamesjoyce.ie. €3.80. Mon.–Sat. 9:30–5, Sun. 12:30–5.*

61 MOUNTJOY SQUARE. Built over the two decades before 1818, this square was once surrounded by elegant, terraced houses, but today only the northern side remains intact. The houses on the once derelict southern side have been converted into apartments. Irishman Brian Boru, who led his soldiers to victory against the Vikings in the Battle of Clontarf in 1014, was said to have pitched camp before the confrontation on the site of Mountjoy Square. Playwright Sean O'Casey once lived at No. 35 and used the square as a setting for *The Shadow of a Gunman*.

53 **O'CONNELL STREET.** Dublin's most famous thoroughfare, 150 ft wide, was previously known as Sackville Street, but its name was changed in 1924, two years after the founding of the Irish Free State. After the devastation of the 1916 Easter Uprising, the street had to be almost entirely reconstructed, a task that took until the end of the 1920s. The main attraction of the street, **Nelson's Pillar,** a Doric column towering over the city center and a marvelous vantage point, was blown up in 1966, the 50th anniversary of the Easter Uprising. The large **monument** at the south end of the street is dedicated to Daniel O'Connell (1775–1847), "The Liberator," and was erected in 1854 as a tribute to the orator's achievement in securing Catholic Emancipation in 1829. Seated winged figures represent the four Victories—courage, eloquence, fidelity, and patriotism—all exemplified by O'Connell. Ireland's four ancient provinces—Munster, Leinster, Ulster, and Connacht—are identified by their respective coats of arms. Look closely and you'll notice that O'Connell is wearing a glove on one hand, as he did for much of his adult life, a self-imposed penance for shooting a man in a duel. Alongside O'Connell is another noted statue, a modern rendition of Joyce's **Anna Livia,** seen as a lady set within a waterfall and now nicknamed by the natives the "floozy in the Jacuzzi." **O'Connell Bridge,** the main bridge spanning the Liffey (wider than it is long), marks the street's southern end.

63 **PRO-CATHEDRAL.** Dublin's principal Catholic cathedral (also known as St. Mary's) was built between 1816 and 1825. Although the severely classical church design is on a suitably epic scale, the building was never granted full cathedral status, nor has the identity of its architect ever been discovered; the only clue is in the church ledger, which lists a "Mr. P." as the builder. The church's facade, with a six-Doric-pillared portico, is based on the Temple of Theseus in Athens; the interior is modeled after the Grecian-Doric style of St-Philippe du Roule in Paris. A Palestrina choir, in which the great Irish tenor John McCormack began his career, sings in Latin here every Sunday at 11. It's still a great place to hear the best Irish male voices. *Marlborough St., tel. 01/874–5441, www.procathedral.ie. Free. Daily 8 AM–6 PM.*

65 **ROTUNDA HOSPITAL.** Founded in 1745 as the first maternity hospital in Ireland or Britain, the Rotunda was designed on a grand scale by architect Richard Castle (1690–1751), with a three-story tower and a copper cupola. It's now most worth a visit for its **chapel**, with elaborate plasterwork executed by Bartholomew Cramillion between 1757 and 1758, appropriately honoring motherhood. The **Gate Theatre,** in a lavish Georgian assembly room, is also part of the complex. The public is not allowed inside. *Parnell St., tel. 01/873–0700.*

62 **ST. FRANCIS XAVIER CHURCH.** One of the city's finest churches in the classical style, the Jesuit St. Francis Xavier was begun in 1829, the year of Catholic Emancipation, and was completed three years later. The building is designed in the shape of a Latin cross, with a distinctive Ionic portico and an unusual coffered ceiling. The striking, faux-marble high altarpiece, decorated with lapis lazuli, came from Italy. The church appears in James Joyce's story "Grace." *Upper Gardiner St., tel. 01/836–3411. Free. Daily 7 AM–8:30 PM.*

ALONG THE GRAND CANAL

At its completion in 1795, the 547-km (342-mi) Grand Canal was celebrated as the longest in Britain and Ireland. It connected Dublin to the River Shannon, and horse-drawn barges carried cargo (mainly turf) and passengers to the capital from all over the country. By the mid-19th century the train had arrived and the great waterway slowly fell into decline, until the last commercial traffic ceased in 1960. But the 6-km (4-mi) loop around the capital is ideal for a leisurely stroll.

Sights to See

71 **BAMBRICK'S.** This is a pub in the best Irish tradition: a long, dark-wood bar, half-empty, frequented mostly by men over 50, with a staff whose sharp, grinning humor borders on being rude. *11 Richmond St. South, tel. 01/475–4402. Free. Daily 11 AM–midnight.*

70 IRISH JEWISH MUSEUM. Though Ireland has never had a large Jewish population (it hovers around 1,800 today), in the late 19th century and early 20th century it did become home to roughly 5,000 European Jews fleeing the pogroms of Eastern Europe. Opened in 1985 by Israeli president Chaim Herzog (himself Dublin-educated), the museum has a restored synagogue and a display of photographs, letters, and personal memorabilia culled from Dublin's most prominent Jewish families, though the exhibits trace the Jewish presence in Ireland back to 1067. In homage to Leopold Bloom, the Jewish protagonist of Joyce's *Ulysses*, every Jewish reference in the novel has been identified. The museum is a 20-minute walk or so from St. Stephen's Green. *3–4 Walworth Rd., tel. 01/453–1797. Free. Oct.–Apr., Sun. 10:30–2:30; May–Sept., Tues., Thurs., and Sun. 11–3:30; also by appointment.*

67 MOUNT STREET BRIDGE. This bridge has a wooden lock on either side and is the perfect spot to watch these original gateways to the canal in operation. On the southwest corner of the bridge a small stone monument commemorates the battle of Mount Street Bridge in 1916 and the Irish Volunteers who died on this spot.

68 SCRUFFY MURPHY'S. Many a backroom deal by the country's political power brokers has been made in the back room of this classy wood-and-brass pub. It's the perfect spot for a pint and a snack. *Lower Mount St., tel. 01/661–50062. Free. Daily 11 AM–midnight.*

69 STATUE OF PATRICK KAVANAGH. Patrick Kavanagh, Ireland's great lyric poet, spent the later years of his life sitting on a bench here writing about the canal, which flowed from his birthplace in the Midlands to the city where he would die. In one such poem he tells those who outlive him, "O commemorate me with no hero-courageous tomb, just a canal-bank seat for the passerby." Acknowledging Kavanagh's devotion to this spot, his friends commissioned a life-size bronze of the poet here. *Canal bank along Wilton Terr.*

66 **WATERWAYS VISITORS CENTRE.** In the airy, wood-and-glass building you can learn about the history of Irish rivers and canals through photos, videos, and models. *Grand Canal Quay, tel. 01/677–7501. €2.55. June–Sept., daily 9:30–5:30; Oct.–May, Wed.–Sun. 12:30–5:30.*

In This Chapter

Revised by Muriel Bolger

eating out

ONCE UPON A TIME, and it wasn't too long ago, dining out in Dublin was a limited pleasure. Even 10 years ago, the city had lots of pubs but few interesting restaurants. All that has changed. With the Irish economy booming, everyone wants to eat out, and, not surprisingly, the Dublin dining scene has exploded with dazzling new places. Growing international interest and a more diverse local palate have also widened the range of restaurants and triggered new developments in Irish cuisine. So if you arrive thinking you're going to be eating potatoes, potatoes, and more potatoes, be prepared to have your preconceptions overturned—and to be very happily sated.

Most Dublin restaurateurs have trained in top restaurants abroad, from France to Switzerland; others have worked in New York and Chicago; and some have been much farther afield—to Thailand, Hong Kong, New Zealand, and Australia. The result is a dizzying choice of restaurants to suit every mood and situation. You can eat superb French or Italian food, often with an Irish twist; you can have all the fusion you want, with menus that experiment with Asian, Mediterranean, and international cuisine; and you'll find plenty of elegant dining rooms, stylish bistros, relaxing hideaways, and late-night eateries to boot.

Irish food is enjoying a renaissance, thanks to talented, imaginative chefs determined to put a fresh spin on traditional ingredients. Organic is the buzzword in Irish cuisine. Fresh produce is being imaginatively treated, too, giving new life to stalwart Irish ingredients such as potatoes, onions, carrots, and cabbage. Seafood, lamb, beef, pork, and bacon still provide the backbone for many signature dishes, but there is also great interest in venison, quail, and other game—both wild and farmed. There are dozens of excellent cheeses—such as St. Tola goat cheese from Clare and Carrigburne Brie from Wexford—most produced by small artisan cheese makers. If one of these farmhouse varieties appears on a menu, make a point of trying it.

Few restaurants in Dublin have dress requirements, but men may feel more comfortable in a jacket and tie at fancier places.

We have included some of the city's best addresses for a hearty pub lunch, a popular dining option among Dubliners.

Prices

Value Added Tax (VAT)—a 12.5% tax on food and a government excise tax on drinks—will automatically be added to your bill. Before paying, check to see whether service has been included. If it has been included, you can pay it with a credit card; but if it has not, it's more considerate to the staff to leave the tip in cash (10% to 15%) if paying the main bill by credit card.

A word of warning—you will pay for your dining pleasure here: high overheads and staffing costs have pushed up prices, especially in more upscale places. The good news is that, although Dublin doesn't have Starbucks, there are scores of local cafés serving excellent coffee, often with a good sandwich.

CATEGORY	COST
$$$$	over €29
$$$	€22–€29
$$	€13–€21
$	under €13

*Per person for a main course at dinner

CENTER CITY (SOUTHSIDE)
AMERICAN

$$$–$$$$ **SHANAHANS.** Dublin's first American-style steak house, in an elegant Georgian building, is proving a huge success. Decor is old-style—think large fireplaces, gilt mirrors, a deep carpet, and elegant chandeliers. Certified Irish Angus beef is the star on the menu, although seafood and lamb feature too. The basement bar—the Oval Office—is full of Americana and presidential paperwork. *119 St. Stephen's Green, tel. 01/407–0939. Reservations essential. AE, DC, MC, V. Closed Sun. No lunch Sat.–Thurs.*

CONTEMPORARY

$$$–$$$$ **PEACOCK ALLEY.** Conrad Gallagher ran away from school at 12
★ to be a cook in his native County Donegal. By 18 he was sous-chef at the Plaza in New York, and at 19 *chef de cuisine* at the Waldorf-Astoria's Peacock Alley, whose name he has borrowed. His elegant, modern restaurant has a large, airy 120-seat room with a spectacular view over St. Stephen's Green at one end and a view of the white-tiled open kitchen at the other. Strikingly inventive dishes include smoked salmon with basmati rice, pear, preserved ginger, soy sauce, and quesadilla; deep-fried crab cakes with *katafi* (shredded phyllo pastry); and daube of pot-roasted beef. The excellent service and strong wine list add to the experience. *Fitzwilliam Hotel, St. Stephen's Green, tel. 01/478–7015. Reservations essential. AE, DC, MC, V. Closed Sun.*

$$–$$$ **COOKE'S CAFÉ.** Johnny Cooke's Mediterranean bistro is a cool spot for visiting movie stars. Sit out in summer under an awning and watch the people go by, enjoying elegantly presented dishes on huge white Wedgwood plates. Favorites here include pasta with a rich bubbling Gorgonzola sauce, lobster simply grilled with garlic-herb butter, salad scattered with pieces of tender roast duck, and crab salad with spinach, coriander, mango salsa, and lime dressing. Try not to be in a hurry, because the service, through charming, is slow. Upstairs is the grill bar Rhino Room, also owned by Cooke. *14 S. William St., tel. 01/679–0536. Reservations essential. AE, DC, MC, V.*

dublin dining

Mao, **28**	101 Talbot, **2**	The Steps of Rome, **33**	**Pub Food**
Mermaid Cafe, **14**	Osteria Romano, **11**	The Tea Room, **4**	Davy Byrne's, **27**
Milano, **35**	Pasta Fresca, **29**	Thornton's, **40**	Old Stand, **23**
Nude, **17**	Patrick Guilbaud, **45**	Wagamama, **34**	O'Neill's, **18**
O'Connells, **48**	Peacock Alley, **30**	Yamamori, **22**	Stag's Head, **16**
Old Dublin, **19**	Shanahans, **39**		Zanzibar, **4**
One Pico, **42**			

\$\$–\$\$\$ **LA STAMPA.** One of the most dramatic dining rooms in Dublin,
★ La Stampa has huge gilt mirrors and elaborate candelabra that
are gloriously over the top and give a sense of occasion to the
simplest meal. The menu changes frequently to reflect an eclectic,
international style. For a main course, you may get rack of organic
lamb with braised beans, tomatoes, and rosemary jus; roast
scallops with artichoke mash and a tomato vinaigrette; or giant
prawns served with garlic or mango mayonnaise. Service is brisk
but friendly, and there's always a fun atmosphere. *35 Dawson St.,
tel. 01/677–8611. AE, DC, MC, V. No lunch.*

CONTINENTAL

\$\$\$–\$\$\$\$ **BROWNES BRASSERIE.** In a Georgian town house on St. Stephen's
Green, now converted to a boutique hotel, this is a lovely spot for
an intimate meal. Huge mirrors reflect the light from crystal
chandeliers, glowing on jewel-color walls and upholstery. The food
is rich and heartwarming, with classics like roast duck breast
served pink with savory sweet corn cake, bittersweet endive, and
coffee bean demi-glace. Treat yourself to the lavender-scented
crème brûlée. *22 St. Stephen's Green, tel. 01/638–3939. Reservations
essential. AE, DC, MC, V. No lunch Sat.*

\$\$\$ **LOCKS.** Claire Douglas's town-house restaurant, overlooking
the Grand Canal, offers a genuinely warm welcome. The dining
room is comfortable and old-fashioned, with banquettes, starched
table linen, and hearty portions served on antique ironstone
plates. Classic starters include Locks's special potato skins—
dished up with prawns, tomato, and spinach, with a fabulous
hollandaise sauce. For the main course, there's a choice of
traditional fish dishes, Irish lamb, and venison. *1 Windsor Terr.,
Portobello, tel. 01/454–3391. Reservations essential. AE, DC, MC, V.
Closed Sun.*

FRENCH

\$\$\$\$ **PATRICK GUILBAUD.** This fine restaurant combines superb French
★ cooking with impeccable service. The best food here is simple but
flawless. Try the house specialty dish, Chalons duck à l'orange. Follow

that if you can with the *assiette au chocolat* (a plate of five different hot and cold chocolate desserts). The walls of the marvelously lofty dining room are hung with paintings from the owners' private collection. *21 Upper Merrion St., tel. 01/676–4192. Reservations essential. AE, DC, MC, V. Closed Sun.–Mon. and late Dec.–mid-Jan.*

$$$$ THORNTON'S. Owner Kevin Thornton is one of the very best
★ chefs in Ireland, and if you are passionate about food, then this place is a must. The upstairs dining room is simply decorated, creating few distractions from the exquisite cuisine. Thornton's cooking style is light, and his dishes are small masterpieces of structural engineering. In season, he marinates legs of partridge, then debones and reforms the bird, with the breasts presented as a crown. Desserts range from banana ice cream to fig tartlet. The enormous selection of cheeses is supplied by Sheridans of Dublin. *1 Portobello Rd., tel. 01/454–9067. Reservations essential. AE, DC, MC, V. Closed Sun.–Mon. No lunch Tues.–Thurs.*

$ LEMON CRÊPE AND COFFEE CO. This is the home of the best crêpes in town, and a new favorite with hungry Dubliners. The space is compact, white, and minimal. There are a few pavement tables— complete with outdoor heater—making this a great spot for a tasty snack while you watch Dublin go by. Savory pancakes can be followed up with sugar-sweet crêpes, and a swift takeout service means you don't have to stop to enjoy good food. *66 S. William St., tel. 01/672–9044. No credit cards.*

INDIAN

$$ JAIPUR. The spacious, contemporary dining room reflects the modern, cutting-edge approach to Indian cooking here. In addition to traditional dishes like chicken *tikka masala* (with spicy tomato sauce) you'll find the more unusual *nizami murgh* (chicken cooked in a white onion and cashew sauce with toasted sesame seeds, pine nuts, and sour cream) on offer. Dishes can be toned down (or heated up!) to suit your palate, and service is courteous and prompt. The wine list is well thought out. *41 S. Great George's St., tel. 01/677–3865. Reservations essential. AE, MC, V.*

$–$$ KHYBER TANDOORI. Just a short walk from St. Stephen's Green is this gem of a tandoori restaurant. Although it specializes in Pakistani cuisine, it serves a broad range of Indian dishes. Try the *shami kebabs* (dainty, spiced patties of minced lamb and lentils) or *kabuli chicken tikka shashlik* (marinated, diced chicken with onions and red and green peppers) that comes bright red and sizzling on an iron platter. Settle in and admire the richly embroidered wall hangings and the great gusts of steam coming from the tandoori oven in the glassed-in area. *44–45 S. William St., tel. 01/670–4855. AE, DC, MC, V. No lunch Sun.*

IRISH

$$$–$$$$ THE COMMONS RESTAURANT. This large, elegant dining room is in the basement of historic Newman House. The patio doors open onto a paved courtyard for summer aperitifs and alfresco lunches. Typical dishes include panfried sea bass with fennel confit, and loin of rabbit with puree of peas, carrot, and rosemary fricassee. If you have time, take a stroll in the Iveagh Gardens, an enclosed park that is one of Dublin's best-kept secrets. *85–86 St. Stephen's Green, tel. 01/478–0530. Reservations essential. AE, DC, MC, V. Closed weekends.*

$$ DOBBINS. Dobbins is popular with businesspeople who like the combination of cozy booth seating, friendly service, and classic bistro food. Owner John O'Byrne presides over an impressive cellar with hundreds of wines from around the world. Tempura of prawns is a popular starter, while boned brace of quail, with black pudding (sausage with dried pig's blood) and foie gras stuffing, is a typical entrée. There is valet parking, and the staff are expert at summoning taxis. *15 Stephens La., off Mount St., tel. 01/676–4679. Reservations essential. AE, DC, MC, V. Closed Sun.–Mon.*

$$ ONE PICO. Although the decor here is traditional in appearance— large fireplaces, swagged windows—Eamonn O'Reilly's cooking is decidedly contemporary. Dishes such as the roast loin of lamb in a soft herb crust, atop a potato-and-bacon gratin with red pepper and thyme, demonstrate a savvy use of Irish ingredients.

Follow this with the baked chèvre cheesecake with praline chocolate and orange confit. Service is excellent, and the top-class cooking makes this good value for money. *1 Upper Camden St., tel. 01/478–0307. Reservations essential. AE, DC, MC, V. No lunch weekends.*

$–$$ THE LORD EDWARD. Creaking floorboards and an old fireplace give the impression of being in someone's drawing room at this establishment, one of the oldest in the city. Start with traditional fish dishes such as smoked salmon, followed by simply cooked Dover sole, salmon, or lobster. Vegetables and potatoes are almost incidental to the fish, but the French fries are excellent. The restaurant is named after Irish revolutionary Lord Edward Fitzgerald, whose remains are buried in St. Werburgh's Church across the road. *23 Christ Church Pl., tel. 01/454–2420. Reservations essential. AE, DC, MC, V. Closed Sun.*

$ BURDOCK'S. Right next door to the Lord Edward is Dublin's famous takeout fish-and-chips shop. Join the inevitable queue and eat in the gardens of St. Patrick's Cathedral, a five-minute walk away. *21 Werburgh St., tel. 01/454–0306. No credit cards.*

$ KILKENNY KITCHEN. On the upper floor of the Kilkenny Shop, this big self-service restaurant is an ideal place to take a break from shopping and sightseeing. Homemade soups, casseroles, cold meats, and salads are arranged on a long buffet, along with lots of tasty breads and cakes. Try to get a table by the window overlooking the playing fields of Trinity College. Lunchtime is busy, but it's very pleasant for morning coffee or afternoon tea. *5–6 Nassau St., tel. 01/677–7066. AE, DC, MC, V.*

ITALIAN

$$–$$$ IL PRIMO. Old wooden tables and chairs give Il Primo a casual feel, and the friendly, if cramped, atmosphere attracts a devoted clientele. The Irish-Italian cuisine is imaginative and reassuring at the same time. Among the main courses, a delicious chicken ravioli in white wine cream with Parma ham and wild mushrooms is a standout. Wine is a specialty here. *Montague St., off Harcourt St., tel. 01/478–3373. AE, DC, MC, V. Closed Sun.*

$–$$ PASTA FRESCA. This stylish little Italian restaurant and deli off Grafton Street squeezes a surprising number of people into a fairly small space. Antipasto *misto* (assorted sliced Italian meats) makes a good appetizer—or go for carpaccio *della casa* (wafer-thin slices of beef fillet, with fresh Parmesan, olive oil, lemon juice, and black pepper). The main courses consist of Pasta Fresca's own very good versions of well-known dishes such as spaghetti *alla Bolognese* (with meat), cannelloni, and lasagna *al forno* (baked). The pasta is freshly made each day. You'll find lines at lunchtime. *3–4 Chatham St., tel. 01/679–2402. AE, DC, MC, V.*

$ MILANO. The big open kitchen at this bright, cheerful place turns out a wide array of tasty, flashy pizzas, with combinations like tomato and mozzarella, ham and eggs, Cajun with prawns and Tabasco, spinach and egg, or ham and anchovies. There are also simple salads, like tomato and mozzarella with dough balls, and a couple of baked pasta dishes. This is a good place to dine late, with last orders at midnight. Two other branches have opened up, one in Temple Bar and another on Bachelors Walk along the Quays. *38 Dawson St., tel. 01/670–7744; 18 Essex St. E, Temple Bar, tel. 01/670–3384; 38–39 Lower Ormond Quay, tel. 01/872–0003. AE, MC, V.*

$ THE STEPS OF ROME. Just a few steps from Grafton Street, it's perfect for a late-night bite or quick lunch. Slices of homemade pizza can be eaten on the spot or wrapped for takeout. The handful of tables is usually full, but it's worth waiting for classic Italian pasta dishes like pasta parmigiano or pesto, and good fresh salads with focaccia. Follow with ice cream or tiramisu and good strong espresso. *1 Chatham Ct., tel. 01/670–5630. No credit cards.*

JAPANESE

$ WAGAMAMA. Modeled on a Japanese canteen, this eatery has long wooden tables and benches ensuring a unique communal dining experience. This low-ceilinged basement noodle bar is constantly packed, but swift service is the key. Formal courses aren't acknowledged: food is served as soon as it's ready, with appetizers and main courses arriving together. Choose from filling bowls of Cha Han (fried rice with chicken, prawns, and vegetables) or chili beef ramen, washed down with a fresh fruit or vegetable juice. S. King St., tel. 01/478–2152. AE, DC, MC, V.

$ YAMAMORI. This is the first of many ramen noodle bars to open in Ireland and one of the best. The meals-in-a-bowl are a splendid slurping experience, and although you will be supplied with a small Chinese-style soup spoon, the best approach is with chopsticks. You can also get authentic sushi and sashimi dishes, as well as delicious chicken teriyaki. 71–72 S. Great George's St., tel. 01/475–5001. AE, DC, MC, V.

PAN-ASIAN

$$–$$$ DIEP LE SHAKER. Slightly off the beaten track, on a narrow lane off Pembroke Street, this big, flamboyant restaurant serving Thai food was an instant success. Comfortable high-back chairs, pristine table linen, and elegant stemware make it a lovely place to dine. Try the steamed scallops and ginger, or lobster in garlic pepper and Thai herbs. Don't be surprised to see people ordering champagne with their meal. There's a permanent party feel that attracts Ireland's new wealthy set in droves. 55 Pembroke La., tel. 01/661–1829. AE, DC, MC, V. Closed Sun.

$–$$ MAO. Everything is Asian fusion at this bustling café, from the little Andy Warhol pastiche of Chairman Mao on the washroom door to the eclectic mix of dishes on the menu, which pay homage to Thai, Vietnamese, and other Southeast Asian cuisines. Favorites are the Malaysian chicken and the Nasi Goreng (Indonesian fried rice with chicken and shrimp). Reservations aren't accepted, so come early to get a seat. There is another branch in Dun Laoghaire, a 20-minute taxi ride from the city center. 2 Chatham Row, tel. 01/670–4899; The Pavilion, Dun Laoghaire, tel. 01/214–8090. MC, V.

RUSSIAN AND SCANDINAVIAN

$$ OLD DUBLIN. Unlikely as it might seem, this brasserie-style restaurant near St. Patrick's Cathedral specializes in Russian and

Scandinavian food. A series of cozy but elegant low-ceilinged rooms are decorated with pristine white linens and candlelit tables and warmed by glowing fires in the evening. Familiar dishes such as blini, borscht, chicken Kiev, and beef Stroganoff feature alongside good Irish staples such as roast lamb and fresh baked salmon. The lunch menu tends to be more conventional, while the evening menu has surprises like planked sirloin Hussar, a steak baked between two oak planks, served on an oak platter with salad and sweet pickle. *90–91 St. Francis St., tel. 01/454–2028. AE, DC, MC, V. Closed Sun. No lunch Sat.*

VEGETARIAN

$ NUDE. This sleek fast-food café was such a good idea that owner Norman Hewson—brother of U2's Bono—has opened another branch for takeout only. The menu is mostly vegetarian, and everything on it is made with organic and free-range ingredients. Choose from homemade soups and vegetable wraps, smoothies, and freshly squeezed juices. *21 Suffolk St., tel. 01/672–5577. MC, V.*

TEMPLE BAR
AMERICAN/CASUAL

$–$$$ BELGO. Part of a chain of Belgian restaurants, it's the perfect place to go if you want a large serving of comfort food and are prepared to be adventurous with what you drink. The menu has dozens of different beers, and the French fries, served alongside omelets, burgers, *saucissons* (large, flavored Belgian sausages), and steaks, are the best you'll eat in Temple Bar. Go early in the evening (between 5:30 and 7:30) and your bill will match the time you arrived. *17–19 Sycamore St., tel. 01/672–7554. AE, DC, MC, V.*

$–$$ ELEPHANT & CASTLE. One of Temple Bar's most popular and established eateries, Elephant & Castle serves up traditional American food—charcoal-grilled burgers, salads, omelets, sandwiches, and pasta. The brunch on Sunday is always packed. The crowds and absence of soft surfaces mean the noise level can be high. When the service is good, the turnover tends to be quick, although you may be inclined to linger, as its formula—an atmosphere that's both bustling *and* relaxed, with generous portions of unfussy and well-prepared food—makes it a casual Dublin standout. New Yorkers take note: yes, this is a cousin of the restaurant of the same name in Greenwich Village. *18 Temple Bar, tel. 01/679–3121. Reservations not accepted. AE, DC, MC, V.*

$ BAD ASS CAFÉ. Sinéad O'Connor used to wait tables at this lively spot in a converted warehouse between the Central Bank and Ha'penny Bridge (a "Rock 'n Stroll" tour plaque notes O'Connor's past here). Old-fashioned cash shuttles whiz around the ceiling of the barnlike space, which has bare floors and is painted in primary colors inside and out. A wall of glass makes for great people-watching. Although the food—mostly pizzas and burgers—is unexceptional, the Bad Ass can be a lot of fun and is popular with appetites of all ages. *9–11 Crown Alley, tel. 01/671–2596. AE, MC, V.*

CONTEMPORARY

$$$–$$$$ THE TEA ROOM. This restaurant is a good place to go if you have something to celebrate or if you're hoping to spot some celebrities: it is part of the Clarence hotel, where stars of stage and screen stay when they're in town. The bright, lofty dining room has spectacular flower arrangements and elegant, modern table settings. The food is adventurous and consistently good. Mouthwatering entrées may include roasted scallops, served with new potatoes and seasonal greens, or grilled corn-fed chicken with goat cheese, pancetta, roasted beetroot, and red onion. *The Clarence, 6–8 Wellington Quay, tel. 01/407–0813. Reservations essential. AE, MC, V.*

$$ MERMAID CAFÉ. One of the chef-owners dabbles in fine art, and a couple of the large canvases on the walls are carried over into painterly bistro cooking. Lunch is an exceptional value—piquant crab cakes, hearty seafood casseroles, venison sausage, or radicchio and melted goats cheese. Good attention to detail and a thoughtful wine list make this modest restaurant with tall windows looking onto busy Dame Street one of the best eateries in Temple Bar. *69 Dame St., tel. 01/670–8236. MC, V.*

$–$$ DISH. Dish has built up a loyal following with its clever cuisine, relaxed dining room, and pleasant staff. The large white room with its sanded floorboards, oversized mirrors, and industrial piping makes a stylish space in which to enjoy Gerard Foote's confident cooking. Dishes range from grilled Clonakilty black pudding with roasted red pepper and borlotti beans to roast monkfish with bacon, savoy cabbage, beetroot, and cream. There is a focus on Irish ingredients. It's popular for Sunday brunch, and the midweek lunch is also excellent value. *2 Crow St., tel. 01/671–1248. Reservations essential. AE, DC, MC, V.*

$–$$ EDEN. The young owners of several of Dublin's café-style bars, ★ including the Front Lounge and the Globe, have followed those successes with a popular brasserie-style restaurant with an open kitchen and high wall of glass looking out onto one of Temple Bar's main squares. Patio-style doors lead to an outdoor eating area—a major plus in a city with relatively few alfresco dining spots. Dishes include duck leg confit with lentils, and braised hock of ham served with mustard crust and *champ* (creamy, buttery mashed potatoes with scallions). For dessert try the rhubarb crème brûlée. *Meeting House Sq., tel. 01/670–5372. Reservations essential. AE, DC, MC, V.*

FRENCH

$$$ LES FRÈRES JACQUES. This restaurant brings a little bit of Paris ★ to Temple Bar: old prints of Paris and Deauville hang on the green-papered walls, and the French waiters, dressed in white Irish linen and black bow ties, exude a Gallic charm without being excessively formal. Expect traditional French cooking that nods to the seasons. Seafood is a major attraction, and lobster, from the tank, is a specialty, typically roasted and flambéed with Irish whiskey. A piano player performs Friday and Saturday evenings and the occasional weeknight. *74 Dame St., tel. 01/679–4555. Reservations essential. AE, DC, MC, V. Closed Sun. No lunch Sat.*

ITALIAN

$ OSTERIA ROMANO. Members of the Italian community congregate in the evenings at this cheerful eatery, dishing up authentic Roman cuisine. Specialties include *melanzane parmigiani*, a delicious dish of baked eggplant and cheese, and the pasta list has excellent cream-based dishes, like spaghetti Alfredo and carbonara. Beware of finishing the meal with too many flaming *sambucas* (anise-flavored, semisweet Italian liqueur). The best table is by the window overlooking the street. 5 *Crow St.*, tel. 01/670–8662. AE, DC, MC, V.

MEDITERRANEAN

$$–$$$ BRUNO'S. Experienced French-born restaurateur Bruno Berta has a hit on his hands with his French-Mediterranean bistro on one of the busiest corners in Temple Bar. Simple but stylish dishes range from starters like *feuilleté* (puff pastry) of crab meat and saffron sauce to main dishes of roasted scallops with Jerusalem artichoke puree and warm smoked bacon and walnut dressing. Friendly service and a relaxed atmosphere make this one of the best bets in the area. 30 *Essex St. E*, tel. 01/670–6767. AE, DC, MC, V. *Closed Sun.*

SOUTH CITY CENTER: BALLSBRIDGE, DONNYBROOK, AND STILLORGAN

CONTEMPORARY

$$ O'CONNELLS. This restaurant puts an emphasis on fresh Irish produce and baked goods. The dining room is a vast, modern space with sleek timber paneling and floor-to-ceiling windows. Go for the spit-roasted chicken or anything baked in the huge clay oven. A huge array of fresh breads is on display in the open kitchen, which turns into a buffet for breakfast and lunch. *Merrion Rd., Ballsbridge*, tel. 01/647–3404. AE, DC, MC, V.

CONTINENTAL

$$–$$$ BEAUFIELD MEWS. A 10-minute taxi ride from the city center, this 18th-century coach house with stables still has its original cobbled courtyard and is even said to be haunted by a friendly monk. Inside it's all black beams, old furniture, and bric-a-brac. The more desirable tables overlook the courtyard or the garden or are, less predictably, "under the nun" (the nun in question is a 17th-century portrait). While the main attraction is the atmosphere, the food is based on fresh ingredients, and you'll find old favorites like roast duckling à l'orange as well as wild-salmon steaks simply grilled. *Woodlands Ave., Stillorgan, tel. 01/288–0375. Reservations essential. AE, DC, MC, V. Closed Mon.*

IRISH

$$–$$$ ERNIE'S RESTAURANT. High-quality ingredients, attention to detail, and consistency are the hallmarks of this long-established restaurant only a few minutes by taxi from the city center. Built around a large tree and fountain, it has a welcoming atmosphere. The seasonal menu always has a variety of catches of the day— grilled sole with spring onion and thyme butter, and poached wild salmon on a bed of creamed potato are examples—as well as meat and poultry entrées such as roasted rack of Wicklow lamb with a caramelized onion tart. *Mulberry Gardens, Donnybrook, tel. 01/269–3300. AE, DC, MC, V. Closed Sun.–Mon. and 1 wk at Christmas. No lunch Sat.*

CITY CENTER (NORTHSIDE)

CONTEMPORARY

$$$$ HALO. This restaurant in the chic Morrison hotel has been an instant hit with the fashion crowd and lawyers from the nearby Four Courts. The dramatic, minimalist dining room with its soaring ceiling looks moody and mysterious by night, and a little forbidding by day. The emphasis is on complex dishes that look as good as they taste: seared, cured salmon on creamed spinach and *pomme vapour* (mashed potatoes) with coriander is a specialty. Desserts are miniature works of art on enormous platters. *The Morrison, Ormond Quay, tel. 01/887–2421. AE, DC, MC, V.*

$$ **CHAPTER ONE.** In the vaulted, stone-walled basement of the Dublin Writers Museum, just down the street from the Hugh Lane Municipal Gallery of Modern Art, this is one of the most notable restaurants in northside Dublin. Try the roast venison with mustard and herb lentils, pancetta and chestnut dumpling, and roasted beetroot. The rich bread-and-butter pudding is a stellar dessert. *18–19 Parnell Sq., tel. 01/873–2266. Reservations essential. AE, DC, MC, V. Closed Sun.–Mon. No lunch Sat.*

$–$$ **HARBOUR MASTER.** The main attraction of this big, airy restaurant and bar in the Irish Financial Services Centre north of the Liffey is its setting overlooking a canal basin. At lunch the place is packed with stockbrokers and lawyers; dinner is more subdued. There's a cavernous bar where you can dine bistro style, but head for the new section, which serves hearty food such as prawn linguine with cashews or beef and Guinness stew. *Custom House Docks, tel. 01/670–1688. AE, DC, MC, V.*

MEDITERRANEAN

$–$$ **101 TALBOT.** Popular with Dublin's art and literary set, and conveniently close to the Abbey and Gate theaters, this comfortable upstairs restaurant showcases an ever-changing exhibition of local artists' work. The menu offers creative contemporary food utilizing fresh, local ingredients. Try the cashew and red-pepper rissoles (fried balls) with chili and ginger jam served with wild and basmati rice. Healthy options and several vegetarian choices make this a highly versatile restaurant. *101 Talbot St., tel. 01/874–5011. Reservations essential. AE, DC, MC, V. Closed Sun.–Mon.*

PUB FOOD

Most pubs serve food at lunchtime, some throughout the day. Dishes range from hearty soups and stews to chicken curries, smoked-salmon salads, and sandwiches, and much of it is surprisingly good. Expect to pay €5–€8 for a main course. Some of the smaller pubs may not take credit cards.

DAVY BYRNE'S. James Joyce immortalized Davy Byrne's in his sprawling novel *Ulysses*. Nowadays it's more akin to a cocktail bar than a Dublin pub, but it's good for fresh and smoked salmon, salads, and a hot daily special. *21 Duke St., tel. 01/671–1298.*

OLD STAND. Conveniently close to Grafton Street, the Old Stand serves grilled food, including steaks. *37 Exchequer St., tel. 01/677–7220.*

O'NEILL'S. This fine pub, a stone's throw from Trinity College, has the best carvery (open from noon to 2:30) of any pub in the city, serving up a hearty lunch for about €6.35–€7.60. *2 Suffolk St., tel. 01/670–5755.*

STAG'S HEAD. With one of Dublin's best pub lunches, the Stag's Head is a favorite of both Trinity students and businesspeople. *1 Dame Ct., tel. 01/679–3701.*

ZANZIBAR. This spectacular and immense bar on the north side of the Liffey looks as though it might be more at home in downtown Marrakesh. While away an afternoon in one of its many wicker chairs and enjoy freshly made sandwiches, salads, and cocktails. *34–35 Lower Ormond Quay, tel. 01/878–7212.*

Eating Well is the Best Revenge

Eating out is a major part of every travel experience. It's a chance to explore flavors you don't find at home. And often the walking you do on vacation means that you can dig in without guilt.

START AT THE TOP By all means take in a really good restaurant or two while you're on the road. A trip is a time to kick back and savor the pleasures of the palate. Read up on the culinary scene before you leave home. Check out representative menus on the Web—some chefs have gone electronic. And ask friends who have just come back. Then reserve a table as far in advance as you can, remembering that the best establishments book up months in advance. Remember that some good restaurants require you to reconfirm the day before or the day of your meal. Then again, some really good places will call you, so make sure to leave a number where you can be reached.

ADVENTURES IN EATING A trip is the perfect opportunity to try food you can't get at home. So leave yourself open to try an ethnic food that's not represented where you live or to eat fruits and vegetables you've never heard of. One of them may become your next favorite food.

BEYOND GUIDEBOOKS You can rely on the restaurants you find in these pages. But also look for restaurants on your own. When you're ready for lunch, ask people you meet where they eat. Look for tiny holes-in-the-wall with a loyal following and the best burgers or crispiest pizza crust. Find out about local chains whose fame rests upon a single memorable dish. There's hardly a food-lover who doesn't relish the chance to share a favorite place. It's fun to come up with your own special find—and asking about food is a great way to start a conversation.

SAMPLE LOCAL FLAVORS Do check out the specialties. Is there a special brand of ice cream or a special dish that you simply must try?

HAVE A PICNIC Every so often eat al fresco. Grocery shopping gives you a whole different view of a place.

In This Chapter

Updated by Anto Howard

shopping

IN DAYS GONE BY, travelers would arrive in Ireland, land of leprechauns, shillelaghs, and shamrocks, and quickly realize that the only known specimens of leprechauns or shillelaghs were those in souvenir-shop windows, while shamrocks mainly bloomed around the borders of Irish linen handkerchiefs and tablecloths. All of this is still true, of course, but today you'll find so much more. The variety and sophistication of stores in Dublin are quite remarkable, as a walk through Dublin's central shopping area, from O'Connell to Grafton Street, proves. Department stores stocking internationally known fashion-designer goods and housewares stand beside small boutiques that make shopping in the city a personalized and pleasurable experience. But don't expect bargains. Prices can be higher in the smaller shops, but the department stores are less likely to stock specifically Irish crafts. Shopping in central Dublin can mean pushing through crowds, especially in the afternoons and on weekends. Most large shops and department stores are open Monday–Saturday 9–6. Although nearly all department stores are closed on Sunday, some smaller specialty shops stay open. Those with later closing hours are noted below. You're particularly likely to find sales in January, February, July, and August.

SHOPPING STREETS

Each of Dublin's dozen or so main shopping streets has a different character, and it's only by visiting them all that you can really appreciate the wide range of items for sale. The main commercial streets north of the river have chain stores and department stores that tend to be less expensive and less design-conscious than their counterparts in the city center on the other side of the Liffey.

City Center (Northside)

HENRY STREET. Running westward from O'Connell Street, this is where cash-conscious Dubliners come to shop. Arnotts department store is the anchor; a host of smaller, specialty stores sells CDs, footwear, and fashion. Henry Street's continuation, Mary Street, has a branch of Marks & Spencer and the Jervis Shopping Centre.

O'CONNELL STREET. One of Dublin's largest department stores, Clery's, faces the GPO across the city's main thoroughfare, which is more downscale than southside city streets but still worth a walk. On the same side of the street as the post office is Eason's, a large book, magazine, and stationery store.

City Center (Southside)

DAWSON STREET. Just east of Grafton Street between Nassau Street to the north and St. Stephen's Green to the south, this is the city's primary bookstore avenue, with Waterstone's and Hodges Figgis facing each other on different sides of the street.

FRANCIS STREET. The Liberties, the oldest part of the city, is the hub of Dublin's antiques trade. This street and surrounding areas, such as the Coombe, have plenty of shops where you can browse. If you're looking for something in particular, dealers will gladly recommend the appropriate store to you.

GRAFTON STREET. Dublin's bustling pedestrian-only main shopping street has two upscale department stores, Marks & Spencer and Brown Thomas. The rest of the street is taken up by smaller shops, many of them branches of international chains such as the Body Shop and Bally, and many British chains. This is also the spot to buy fresh flowers, available at reasonable prices from a number of outdoor stands. Smaller streets off Grafton Street, especially Duke Street, South Anne Street, and Chatham Street, have worthwhile crafts, clothing, and designer housewares shops.

NASSAU STREET. Dublin's main tourist-oriented thoroughfare has some of the best-known stores selling Irish goods, but you won't find many locals shopping here. Still, if you're looking for classic Irish gifts to take home, you should be sure at least to browse along here.

TEMPLE BAR. Dublin's hippest neighborhood is dotted with small, precious boutiques—mostly intimate, quirky shops that traffic in a small selection of *très* trendy goods, from vintage wear to some of the most avant-garde Irish clothing you'll find anywhere in the city.

SPECIALTY SHOPPING CENTERS

City Center (Northside)

ILAC CENTRE (Henry St.) was Dublin's first large, modern shopping center, with two department stores, hundreds of specialty shops, and several restaurants. The stores are not as exclusive as at some of the other centers, but there's plenty of free parking.

The **JERVIS SHOPPING CENTRE** (Jervis and Mary Sts., tel. 01/878–1323) has the major British chain stores. It has a compact design and plenty of parking space.

City Center (Southside)

POWERSCOURT TOWNHOUSE CENTRE (59 S. William St.), the former town home of Lord Powerscourt and built in 1771, has an interior courtyard that has been refurbished and roofed over; a

dublin shopping

pianist often plays on the dais at ground-floor level. Coffee shops and restaurants share space with a mix of antiques and crafts stores, including the **HQ Gallery,** the main showcase of the Irish Craft Council and one of the finest places in Dublin to buy contemporary crafts. You can also buy original Irish fashions here by young designers like Gráinne Walsh.

ROYAL HIBERNIAN WAY (Off Dawson St. between S. Anne and Duke Sts., tel. 01/679–5919) is on the former site of the two-centuries-old Royal Hibernian Hotel, a coaching inn that was demolished in 1983. The stylish shops are small in scale and include a branch of Leonidas, the Belgian chocolate firm.

ST. STEPHEN'S GREEN CENTRE (Northwest corner of St. Stephen's Green, tel. 01/478–0888), Dublin's largest and most ambitious shopping center, resembles a giant greenhouse, with ironwork in the Victorian style. On three floors overlooked by a vast clock, the 100 mostly small shops sell a variety of crafts, fashions, and household goods.

TOWER DESIGN CENTRE (Pearse St., tel. 01/677–5655), east of the heart of the city center (near the Waterways Visitor Centre), has more than 35 separate crafts shops in a converted 1862 sugar-refinery tower. On the ground floor, you can stop at workshops devoted to heraldry and Irish pewter; the other six floors feature hand-painted silks, ceramics, hand-knit items, jewelry, and fine-art cards and prints.

WESTBURY MALL (Westbury Hotel, off Grafton St.) is an upmarket shopping mall, with stores selling designer jewelry, antique rugs, and decorative goods.

County Dublin Suburbs

BLACKROCK (Blackrock, Co. Dublin, tel. 01/283–1660), to the south, is technically outside of Dublin's city center, but it deserves special mention as one of the most customer-friendly shopping centers around. It's built on two levels, looking onto an inner courtyard, with the giant Superquinn Foodstore, cafés, and restaurants. Blackrock can be reached conveniently on the DART train line; it has its own stop.

BLANCHARDSTOWN (Blanchardstown, Dublin 15, tel. 01/822–1356) is the biggest shopping center in the country. It's a good spot for bargains and a chance to see Dublin families about their everyday lives. The No. 39 bus from Lower Abbey Street goes to Blanchardstown.

DEPARTMENT STORES

ARNOTTS (Henry St., tel. 01/872–1111) has a wide variety of clothing, household, and sporting goods filling three complete floors; the smaller Grafton Street branch (Grafton St., tel. 01/872–1111) stocks only new fashion and footwear.

A-WEAR (Grafton St., tel. 01/671–7200; Henry St., tel. 01/872–4644) is a line of shops specializing in fashion for men and women. Many of the items are seasonal and closely follow the ever-changing styles. A steady stream of clothing is supplied by leading Irish designers, including John Rocha.

BROWN THOMAS (Grafton St., tel. 01/679–5666), Dublin's most exclusive department store, stocks the leading designer names in clothing and cosmetics and a wide variety of stylish accessories. It also carries clothing by Irish designers.

CLERY'S (O'Connell St., tel. 01/878–6000) was once the city's most fashionable department store and is still worth a visit, despite its rapidly aging decor. It has four floors of all types of merchandise—from fashion to home appliances—and caters to a distinctly modest, traditional sense of style.

DUNNES STORES (St. Stephen's Green Centre, tel. 01/478–0188; Henry St., tel. 01/872–6833; Ilac Shopping Center, Mary

St., tel. 01/873–0211) is Ireland's largest chain of department stores. All stores stock fashion, household, and grocery items and have a reputation for value and variety.

EASON'S (O'Connell St., tel. 01/873–3811; Ilac Shopping Center, Mary St., tel. 01/872–1322) is known primarily for its wide variety of books, magazines, and stationery; its larger O'Connell Street branch now sells tapes, CDs, records, videos, and other audiovisual goodies.

MARKS & SPENCER (Grafton St., tel. 01/679–7855; Henry St., tel. 01/872–8833), perennial competitor to Brown Thomas, stocks everything from fashion (including lingerie) to tasty, unusual groceries. The Grafton Street branch even has its own bureau de change, which doesn't charge commission.

ROCHES STORES (Henry St., tel. 01/873–0044) is where sensible Dubliners have shopped for generations. Household goods are the specialty, but you'll find great value on clothes as well.

OUTDOOR MARKETS

Dublin has a number of open-air markets. **MOORE STREET,** behind the Ilac center, is open Monday–Saturday 9–6. Stalls lining both sides of the street sell fruits and vegetables; it's also a good spot to come to buy shoes and boots. The traditional Dublin repartee here is renowned in the city. Other open markets are only open on weekends. A variety of bric-a-brac is sold at the **LIBERTY MARKET** on the north end of Meath Street, open on Friday and Saturday 10–6, Sunday noon–5:30. The outdoor **MEETING HOUSE SQUARE MARKET** is held every Saturday morning at the heart of Temple Bar. Homemade foodstuffs from breads to chocolate to organic veggies are on offer at a price. Outside the city center, weekend markets take place in Blackrock and Dun Laoghaire.

SPECIALTY SHOPS

Antiques

Dublin is one of Europe's best cities in which to buy antiques, largely due to a long and proud tradition of restoration and high-quality craftsmanship. The Liberties, Dublin's oldest district, is fittingly the hub of the antiques trade and is chock-a-block with shops and traders. Bachelor's Walk, along the quays, also has some decent shops. Although the economic boom has created quite a seller's market, bargains are still possible.

ANTIQUES AND COLLECTIBLES FAIRS (tel. 01/670–8295) take place at Newman House (85–86 St. Stephen's Green) every second Sunday throughout the year.

CONLON ANTIQUES (21 Clanbrassil St., tel. 01/453–7323) has a wide selection of antiques, from sideboards to fanlights.

HA'PENNY BRIDGE GALLERIES (15 Bachelor's Walk, tel. 01/872–3950) has four floors of curios, with a particularly large selection of bronzes, silver, and china.

O'SULLIVAN ANTIQUES (43–44 Francis St., tel. 01/454–1143 or 01/453–9659) specializes in 18th- and 19th-century furniture and has a high-profile clientele, including Mia Farrow and Liam Neeson.

Books

You won't have any difficulty weighing down your suitcase with books: Ireland, after all, produced four Nobel literature laureates in just under 75 years. If you're at all interested in modern and contemporary literature, be sure to leave yourself time to browse through the bookstores, as you're likely to find books available here you can't find back home. Best of all, thanks to an enlightened national social policy, there's no tax on books, so if you only buy books, you don't have to worry about getting VAT slips.

BOOKS UPSTAIRS (36 College Green, tel. 01/679–6687) carries an excellent range of special-interest books, including gay and feminist literature, psychology, and self-help books.

CATHACH BOOKS (10 Duke St., tel. 01/671–8676) sells first editions of Irish literature and many other books of Irish interest, plus old maps of Dublin and Ireland.

DUBLIN BOOKSHOP (24 Grafton St., tel. 01/677–5568) is an esteemed, family-owned bookstore.

FRED HANNA'S (29 Nassau St., tel. 01/677–1255) sells old and new books, with a good choice of works on travel and Ireland.

GREENE'S (Clare St., tel. 01/676–2544) carries an extensive range of secondhand volumes.

HODGES FIGGIS (56–58 Dawson St., tel. 01/677–4754), Dublin's leading independent, stocks 1½ million books on three floors; there's also a pleasant café on the first floor.

HUGHES & HUGHES (St. Stephen's Green Centre, tel. 01/478–3060) has strong travel and Irish-interest sections. There is also a store at Dublin Airport.

WATERSTONE'S (7 Dawson St., tel. 01/679–1415), a large branch of the British chain, has two floors featuring a fine selection of Irish and international books.

WINDING STAIR (40 Ormond Quay, Dublin 1, tel. 01/873–3292) is a charming new- and used-book store overlooking the Liffey. The little upstairs café is the perfect spot for an afternoon of reading.

China, Crystal, Ceramics, and Jewelry

Ireland is synonymous with Waterford crystal, which is available in a wide range of products, including relatively inexpensive items. But other lines are now gaining recognition, such as Cavan, Galway, and Tipperary crystal. **BROWN THOMAS** is the best department store for crystal; the best specialty outlets are listed below.

BLARNEY WOOLLEN MILLS (21–23 Nassau St., tel. 01/671–0068) is one of the best places for Belleek china, Waterford and Galway crystal, and Irish linen.

CRAFTS CENTRE OF IRELAND (Stephen's Green Centre, tel. 01/475–4526) has an impressive inventory of Ireland's most famous contemporary designers, including Michael Kennedy and Diane McCormick (ceramics), Glen Lucas (wood turning), and Jerpoint Glass (glassworks).

CRANNÓG (Crown Alley, tel. 01/671–0805), in Temple Bar, specializes in ceramics and contemporary Irish jewelry, especially silver pendants and rings.

DESIGNYARD (E. Essex St., tel. 01/677–8453) carries beautifully designed Irish and international tableware, lighting, small furniture, and jewelry.

HOUSE OF IRELAND (37–38 Nassau St., tel. 01/671–6133) has an extensive selection of crystal, jewelry, tweeds, sweaters, and other upscale goods.

KILKENNY SHOP (5–6 Nassau St., tel. 01/677–7066) specializes in contemporary Irish-made ceramics, pottery, and silver jewelry and also holds regular exhibits of exciting new work by Irish craftspeople.

MCDOWELL (3 Upper O'Connell St., tel. 01/874–4961), a jewelry shop popular with Dubliners, has been in business for more than 100 years.

TIERNEYS (St. Stephen's Green Centre, tel. 01/478–2873) carries a good selection of crystal and china. Claddagh rings, pendants, and brooches are popular buys.

WEIR & SONS (96 Grafton St., tel. 01/677–9678), Dublin's most prestigious jewelers, sells a wide range of goods in addition to jewelry and watches, including china, glass, lamps, silver, and leather.

Museum Stores

NATIONAL GALLERY OF IRELAND SHOP (Merrion Sq. W, tel. 01/678–5450) has a terrific selection of books on Irish art, plus posters, postcards, note cards, and a wide array of lovely bibelots.

NATIONAL MUSEUM SHOP (Kildare St., tel. 01/677–7444 ext. 327) carries jewelry based on ancient Celtic artifacts in the museum collection, contemporary Irish pottery, a large selection of books, and other gift items.

TRINITY COLLEGE LIBRARY SHOP (Old Library, Trinity College, tel. 01/608–2308) sells Irish-theme books, Book of Kells souvenirs of all kinds, plus clothing, jewelry, and other lovely Irish-made items.

Music

An increasing amount of Irish-recorded material—including traditional folk music, country-and-western, rock, and even a smattering of classical music—is available.

CELTIC NOTE (12 Nassau St., tel. 01/670–4157) is aimed at the tourist market, with a lot of compilations and greatest hits formats.

CLADDAGH RECORDS (2 Cecilia St., tel. 01/679–3664) has a good selection of traditional and folk music.

GAEL LINN (26 Merrion Sq., tel. 01/676–7283) specializes in traditional Irish-music and Irish-language recordings; it's where the aficionados shop.

HMV (65 Grafton St., tel. 01/679–5334; 18 Henry St., tel. 01/872–2095) is one of the larger record shops in town.

MCCULLOGH PIGGOTT (25 Suffolk St., tel. 01/677–3138) is the best place in town for instruments, sheet music, scores, and books about music.

TOWER RECORDS (6–8 Wicklow St., tel. 01/671–3250) is the best-stocked international chain.

VIRGIN MEGASTORE (14–18 Aston Quay, tel. 01/677–7361) is Dublin's biggest music store and holds in-store performances by Irish bands.

Sweaters and Tweeds

If you think Irish woolens are limited to Aran sweaters and tweed jackets, you'll be pleasantly surprised by the range of hats, gloves, scarves, blankets, and other goods you can find. If you're traveling outside of Dublin, you may want to wait to make purchases elsewhere, but if Dublin is it, you still have plenty of good shops to choose from. The tweed on sale in Dublin comes from two main sources, Donegal and Connemara; labels inside the garments guarantee authenticity. The following are largest retailers of traditional Irish woolen goods in the city.

AN TÁIN (13 Temple Bar Sq. N, tel. 01/679–0523) carries hyperstylish handmade Irish sweaters, jackets, and accessories.

BLARNEY WOOLLEN MILLS (21–23 Nassau St., tel. 01/671–0068) has a good selection of tweed, linen, and woolen sweaters in all price ranges.

CLEO LTD. (18 Kildare St., tel. 01/676–1421) sells hand-knit sweaters and accessories made only from natural fibers; it also carries its own designs.

DUBLIN WOOLLEN MILLS (Metal Bridge Corner, tel. 01/677–5014) at Ha'penny Bridge has a good selection of hand-knit and other woolen sweaters at competitive prices.

KEVIN AND HOWLIN (31 Nassau St., tel. 01/677–0257) specializes in handwoven tweed men's jackets, suits, and hats and also sells tweed fabric.

MONAGHAN'S (Grafton Arcade, 15–17 Grafton St., tel. 01/677–0823) specializes in cashmere.

Vintage Clothing

FLIP (4 Upper Fownes St., tel. 01/671–4299), one of the original stores in Temple Bar, sells vintage and retro clothing from the '50s, '60s, and '70s.

JENNY VANDER (Georges Street Arcade, tel. 01/677–0406) is the most famous name in Irish vintage and retro clothing. Just browsing through her collection is a pleasure.

In This Chapter

Updated by Anto Howard

outdoor activities and sports

HEALTH CLUBS ARE RELATIVELY NEW to the city, but they are starting to flourish (especially at hotels). Yet there are plenty of other ways to get out and move about. You can explore a beach; cheer on a hometown team; or walk, run, horseback ride, or bike through Phoenix Park.

BEACHES

To the north of Dublin city is **NORTH BULL ISLAND,** created over the years by the action of the tides and offering an almost 3-km-long (2-mi-long) stretch of fine sand. Bus 130 from Lower Abbey Street stops by the walkway to the beach. **MALAHIDE,** a charming village on the northside DART line, has a clean and easily accessible beach, though the current can be strong. The main beach for swimming on the south side of Dublin is at **KILLINEY** (13 km [8 mi] south of the city center), a shingle (pebbly) beach stretching for 3 km (2 mi). The DART train station is right by the beach; the stop is called Killiney. Near Dublin city center, **SANDYMOUNT STRAND** is a long expanse of fine sand where the tide goes out nearly 3 km (2 mi), but it's not suitable for swimming or bathing because the tide races in so fast. The strand can be reached easily by the DART train.

PARTICIPANT SPORTS

If it's essential that you get in a daily workout, you should be able to do so while you're in Dublin, although it will probably take some careful planning. Check the service information provided for each hotel for particular fitness amenities; if none are listed, call to inquire, as many of the hotels are adding these amenities.

Bicycling

Bicycling is not recommended in the city center, as traffic is heavy and most roads don't have shoulders, much less bike lanes. Phoenix Park and some suburbs (especially Ballsbridge, Clontarf, and Sandymount), however, are pleasant for biking once you're off the main roads. To the immediate south of Dublin, the Dublin and Wicklow mountains provide plenty of challenging terrain. Care should always be taken in securing your bicycle when it's left unattended.

Bicycles can be rented for about €57.15 a week, with an equivalent amount charged for deposit. Nearly 20 companies in the Dublin region rent bicycles; Tourist Information Offices (TIOs) have a full list. **MCDONALD'S** (38 Wexford St., tel. 01/ 475–2586) is a centrally located bike repair and rental shop. **MIKE'S BIKE SHOP** (Dun Laoghaire Shopping Center, tel. 01/ 280–0417) is a traditional bike outfit in the southside suburbs of Dublin. **TRACKS CYCLES** (8 Botanic Rd., Glasnevin, tel. 01/873– 2455) has an established reputation for repair, sales, and rental of all types of bikes.

Bowling

Bowling is a popular sport in Dublin; two kinds are played locally. The sedate, outdoor variety known as crown-green bowling is played at a number of locations in the suburbs. **HERBERT PARK** (Ballsbridge, tel. 01/660–1875) has a splendid, baby-soft bowling green. **KENILWORTH BOWLING CLUB** (Grosvenor Sq., tel. 01/497–2305) welcomes paying visitors, and lessons are available. Dublin has six indoor, 10-pin bowling centers. **BRAY BOWL** (Quinsboro Rd., tel. 01/286–4455) is a bowling center that serves the area near the Wicklow border. **LEISUREPLEX COOLOCK** (Malahide Rd., tel. 01/848–5722; Village Green Center, Tallaght, tel. 01/459–9411) is a mecca for bowlers from both sides of the city. **METRO BOWL** (149 N. Strand Rd., tel. 01/855–0400) tends to attract the more serious bowlers. **STILLORGAN BOWL** (Stillorgan, tel. 01/288–1656) is the oldest 10-pin center in Ireland. **SUPERDOME** (Palmerstown, tel. 01/626–0700) draws big crowds of teenage and family bowlers.

Golf

The Dublin region is an idyllic place for golfers, with more than 30 18-hole courses and 16 9-hole courses and several more on the way. **DEER PARK** (Howth, tel. 01/832–6039) is a top-quality parkland golf course. **EDMONSTOWN** (Rathfarnham, tel. 01/493–2461) is a beautiful golf course with an upmarket clientele. **ELM PARK** (Donnybrook, tel. 01/269–3438) welcomes visiting golfers and beginners. **FOXROCK** (Torquay Rd., tel. 01/289–3992) is a tough golf course with a gorgeous location in the southside suburbs. **HERMITAGE** (Lucan, tel. 01/626–4781) is one of the city's more difficult golf courses. **NEWLANDS** (Clondalkin, tel. 01/459–2903) attracts golfers from all over the northside of the city. **SUTTON** (Sutton, tel. 01/832–3013) golf course is as exclusive and as pricey as everything else in this wealthy suburb. **WOODBROOK** (Bray, tel. 01/282–4799) is worth the trip out of the city for a day's golf by the sea.

The **VIRTUAL GOLF COURSE** (Cow St., tel. 01/672–6181) in Temple Bar allows you to practice even if it's raining. You strike a real ball with a real club against a huge screen, which tracks the virtual course of your shot. Thirty-four of the world's most famous courses can be played, including St. Andrews and

Pebble Beach. It costs €19.05 for a half hour, and you must book ahead.

Health Clubs

The health craze has reached laconic Dublin, and health clubs are springing up all over the city. The **IVEAGH FITNESS CLUB** (Christ Church St., Dublin 8, tel. 01/454–6555) is next to Christ Church Cathedral, in beautiful old redbrick buildings. It has a pool, sauna, and full weight room. Just off Grafton Street, the **JACKIE SKELLY FITNESS CENTRE** (41–42 Clarendon St., Dublin 2, tel. 01/677–0040) is perfect if you're staying in a city-center hotel without a gym.

Horseback Riding

Dublin's environs are excellent for horseback riding. Stables on the city outskirts give immediate access to suitable riding areas. In the city itself, Phoenix Park provides superb, quiet riding conditions away from the busy main road that bisects the park. About 20 riding stables in the greater Dublin area have horses for hire by the hour or the day, for novices and experienced riders; a few also operate as equestrian centers and have lessons. **BRITTAS LODGE RIDING STABLES** (Brittas, tel. 01/458–2726) have fantastic facilities and a setting right beside one of the East Coast's nicest beaches. Horseback riders at the **DEERPARK RIDING CENTER** (Castleknock Rd., Castleknock, tel. 01/820–7141) canter in Dublin's massive Phoenix Park. Outside Dublin, Counties Dublin, Kildare, Louth, Meath, and Wicklow all have unspoiled country territory ideal for horseback riding.

Jogging

Traffic in Dublin is heavy from early morning until late into the night and it's getting worse, so if you're used to jogging the streets back home be aware that here you'll have to dodge vehicles and stop for lights. (Remember *always* to look to your right *and* your left before crossing a street.) If you're staying in Temple Bar or on the western end of the city and you can run 9 km (5½ mi) head to Phoenix Park, easily the nicest place in the city for a jog. If you're on the southside, Merrion Square, St. Stephen's Green, and Trinity College are all good places for short jogs, though be prepared to dodge pedestrians; if you're looking for a longer route, ask your hotel to direct you to the Grand Canal, which has a pleasant path you can run along as far east as the Grand Canal Street Bridge.

Swimming

Dublin has 12 public pools. One of the best is **TOWNSEND STREET** (Townsend St., tel. 01/677–0503). **WILLIAMS PARK** (Rathmines, tel. 01/496–1275) is a quality public pool located on the southside. **DUNDRUM FAMILY RECREATION CENTER** (Meadowbrook, Dundrum, tel. 01/298–4654) is a private pool open to the public for a small fee. **FITZPATRICK CASTLE HOTEL** (Killiney, tel. 01/285–0328) has a pool in its beautiful grounds. **ST. VINCENT'S** (Navan Rd., tel. 01/838–4906) is a public pool on the northside of the city. **TERENURE COLLEGE** (Templeogue Rd., tel. 01/490–7071) is a high school with a pool that's open to the public sometimes. For a hardy dip, there's year-round sea swimming at the **FORTY FOOT BATHING POOL,** a traditional bathing area in Sandycove.

Tennis

Tennis is one of Dublin's most popular participant sports, and some public parks have excellent tennis facilities open to the public. **BUSHY PARK** (Terenure, tel. 01/490–0320) has well-maintained public tennis courts. **HERBERT PARK** (Ballsbridge, tel. 01/668–4364) attracts some serious tennis players with its excellent facilities. **ST. ANNE'S PARK** (Dollymount Strand, tel. 01/

833–8898) has quality tennis courts within sniffing distance of the ocean. Several private tennis clubs are open to the public. **KILTERNAN TENNIS CENTRE** (Kilternan Golf and Country Club Hotel, Kilternan, tel. 01/295–3729) has everything the tennis player could want—at a price. **LANSDOWNE LAWN TENNIS CLUB** (Londonbridge Rd., Dublin 4, tel. 01/668–0219) is as much about the social gathering as it is about the game itself. Dress appropriately. **WEST WOOD LAWN TENNIS CLUB** (Leopardstown Racecourse, Foxrock, Dublin 18, tel. 01/289–2911) is popular with young, serious-minded players. For more information, contact **TENNIS IRELAND** (22 Argyle Sq., Donnybrook, Dublin 4, tel. 01/668–1841).

SPECTATOR SPORTS

Gaelic Games

The traditional games of Ireland, Gaelic football and hurling, attract a huge following, with roaring crowds cheering on their county teams. Games are held at Croke Park, the national stadium for Gaelic games, just north of the city center. For details of matches, contact the **GAELIC ATHLETIC ASSOCIATION (GAA)** (Croke Park, tel. 01/836–3222). The **GAELIC ATHLETIC ASSOCIATION MUSEUM** (New Stand, Croke Park, tel. 01/855–8176, www.gaa.ie; €3.80; May–Sept., daily 9:30–5; Oct.–Apr., Tues.–Sat. 10–5, Sun. noon–5) has high-tech displays about the history of Gaelic games, with plenty of footage from famous games. Exhibits also explain the key link between Gaelic Games and the emergence of the Irish nation.

Greyhound Racing

As elsewhere in the world, greyhound racing is a sport in decline in Ireland. But the track can still be one of the best places to see Dubliners at their most passionate, among friends, and full of wicked humor. **HAROLDS CROSS** (Harolds Cross, Dublin 6, tel.

01/497–1081) is a dilapidated greyhound racing track but serves its purpose. **SHELBOURNE PARK** (Shelbourne Park, Dublin 4, tel. 01/668–3502) is a relatively stylish place to watch greyhound racing. You can book a table in the restaurant overlooking the track.

Horse Racing

Horse racing—from flat to hurdle to steeplechase—is one of the great sporting loves of the Irish. The sport is closely followed and betting is popular, but the social side of attending racing is also important to Dubliners. The main course in Dublin is **LEOPARDSTOWN** (tel. 01/289–3607), an ultramodern course on the southside and home of the Hennessey Gold Cup held in February, Ireland's most prestigious steeplechase. **FAIRYHOUSE** (Co. Meath, tel. 01/825–6167) hosts the Grand National, the most popular steeplechase of the season, every Easter Monday. The **CURRAGH** (tel. 045/441205), southwest of Dublin, hosts the five Classics, the most important flat races of the season, which are run from May to September. **PUNCHESTOWN** (tel. 045/897704), outside Naas, County Kildare, is home of the ever-popular Punchestown National Hunt Festival in April.

Rugby

International rugby matches are staged during the winter and spring at the vast **LANSDOWNE ROAD STADIUM.** Local matches are played every weekend, also in winter and spring. For details, contact the **IRISH RUGBY FOOTBALL UNION** (62 Lansdowne Rd., tel. 01/668–4601).

Soccer

Although soccer—called football in Europe—is very popular in Ireland (largely due to the euphoria resulting from the national team's successes throughout the late 1980s and early '90s), facilities for watching it are not so ideal; they tend to be small and out-of-date. **LANSDOWNE ROAD,** the vast rugby stadium, is the main center for international matches. League of Ireland soccer matches take place throughout the city every Sunday from September to May. For details, contact the **FOOTBALL ASSOCIATION OF IRELAND** (80 Merrion Sq. S, tel. 01/676–6864).

Distance Conversion Chart

Kilometers/Miles

To change kilometers (km) to miles (mi), multiply km by .621.
To change mi to km, multiply mi by 1.61.

km to mi	mi to km
1 = .62	1 = 1.6
2 = 1.2	2 = 3.2
3 = 1.9	3 = 4.8
4 = 2.5	4 = 6.4
5 = 3.1	5 = 8.1
6 = 3.7	6 = 9.7
7 = 4.3	7 = 11.3
8 = 5.0	8 = 12.9

Meters/Feet

To change meters (m) to feet (ft), multiply m by 3.28.
To change ft to m, multiply ft by .305.

m to ft	ft to m
1 = 3.3	1 = .30
2 = 6.6	2 = .61
3 = 9.8	3 = .92
4 = 13.1	4 = 1.2
5 = 16.4	5 = 1.5
6 = 19.7	6 = 1.8
7 = 23.0	7 = 2.1
8 = 26.2	8 = 2.4

In This Chapter

Updated by Anto Howard

nightlife and the arts

Long before Stephen Daedalus's excursions into nighttown (read Joyce's *A Portrait of the Artist as a Young Man*), Dublin was proud of its lively after-hours scene, particularly its thriving pubs. Lately, however, with the advent of Irish rock superstars (think U2, the Cranberries, Sinéad O'Connor, Bob Geldof) and the resurgence of Celtic music (think *Riverdance*, the sound track to *Titanic*), the rest of the world seems to have discovered that Dublin is one of the most happening places in the world. Most nights the city's pubs and clubs overflow with young cell phone–toting Dubliners and Europeans who descend on the capital for weekend getaways. The city's 900-plus pubs are its main source of entertainment; many public houses in the city center have live music—from rock to jazz to traditional Irish.

A number of newspapers have informative listings: the *Irish Times* has a daily guide to what's happening in Dublin and in the rest of the country, as well as complete film and theater schedules. The *Evening Herald* lists theaters, cinemas, and pubs with live entertainment. *In Dublin* and the *Big Issue* are weekly guides to all film, theater, and musical events around the city. The *Event Guide*, a weekly free paper that lists music, cinema, theater, art shows, and dance clubs, can be found in pubs and cafés around the city. In peak season, consult the free Bord Fáilte leaflet "Events of the Week."

NIGHTLIFE

Dubliners have always enjoyed a night out, but in the last decade or so they have turned the pleasure into a work of art.

The city has undergone a major nightlife revolution and now, for better or worse, bears more than a passing resemblance to Europe's nightclub mecca, London. The old-fashioned discos, once the only alternative for late-night entertainment, have been replaced by a plethora of internationally known dance clubs where style and swagger rule. The streets of the city center, once hushed after the pubs had closed, are the scene of what appears to be a never-ending party; indeed, you're as likely to find crowds at 2 AM on a Wednesday as you are at the same time on a Saturday. Although the majority of clubs cater to an under-30 crowd of trendy students and young professionals eager to sway to the rhythmic throb of electronic dance music, there are plenty of alternatives, including a number of nightclubs where the dominant sounds range from soul to salsa. And if you're looking for something less strenuous, Dublin doesn't disappoint: there are brasseries, bistros, cafés, and all manner of other late-night eateries where you can sit, sip, and chat until 2 AM or later.

In another trend, some of Dublin's old classic pubs—arguably some of the finest watering holes in the world—have been "reinvented" as popular spots, with modern interiors and designer drinks to attract a younger, upwardly mobile crowd. Despite the changes, however, the traditional pub has steadfastly clung to its role as the primary center of Dublin's social life. The city has nearly 1,000 pubs ("licensed tabernacles," writer Flann O'Brien calls them). And while the vision of elderly men enjoying a chin wag over a creamy pint of stout has become something of a rarity, there are still plenty of places where you can enjoy a quiet drink and a chat. Last drinks are called as late as 12:30 AM Monday to Saturday and 11 PM on Sunday; some city-center pubs even have extended opening hours from Thursday through Saturday and don't serve last drinks until 1:45 AM.

A word of warning: although most pubs and clubs are extremely safe, the lads can get lively—public drunkenness is very much a part of Dublin's nightlife. While this is for the most part seen as the Irish form of unwinding after a long week (or day!), it can sometimes lead to regrettable incidents such as fighting. In an effort to keep potential trouble at bay, bouncers and security men maintain a visible presence in all clubs and many pubs around the city. At the end of the night, the city center is full of young people trying to get home, which makes for extremely long lines at taxi stands and late-night bus stops, especially on weekends. The combination of drunkenness and impatience can sometimes lead to trouble, so act cautiously. If you need late-night transportation, try to arrange it with your hotel before you go out.

Pubs

SOUTH CITY CENTER

BYRNES (Galloping Green, Stillorgan, tel. 01/288–7683) has the airy atmosphere of an old-fashioned country pub, even though it's only 8 km (5 mi) from the city center. It's one of the few pubs that haven't been renovated.

DUBLINER PUB (Jurys hotel, Pembroke Rd., Ballsbridge, tel. 01/660–5000) has been remade as an old-fashioned Irish pub; it's a busy meeting place during lunch and after work.

JOHN FALLONS (129 Dean St.), a classy public house in the Liberties, has one of the finest snugs in the city and great photos of old Dublin.

KIELY'S (Donnybrook Rd., tel. 01/283–0208) appears at first glance to be just another modernized pub, but go up the side lane and you'll find a second pub, Ciss Madden's, in the same building. Even though it was built in 1992, it's an absolutely authentic and convincing reconstruction of an ancient Irish tavern, right down to the glass globe lights and old advertising signs.

KITTY O'SHEA'S (Upper Grand Canal St., tel. 01/660–9965) has Pre-Raphaelite–style stained glass, complementing its lively, sports-oriented atmosphere. Its sister pubs are in Brussels and Paris; this is the original.

O'BRIEN'S (Sussex Terr., tel. 01/668–2594), beside the Doyle Burlington hotel, is a little antique gem of a pub, scarcely changed in 50 years, with traditional snugs.

CITY CENTER

BRAZEN HEAD (Bridge St., tel. 01/677–9549), Dublin's oldest pub (the site has been licensed since 1198), has stone walls and open fires that have changed little over the years. It's renowned for traditional-music performances and for lively sing-along sessions on Sunday evenings. A little difficult to find, the Brazen Head is on the south side of the Liffey quays; turn down Lower Bridge Street, and then make a right into the old lane.

CAFÉ-EN-SEINE (40 Dawson St., tel. 01/677–4369) is a Parisian-style "locale," with a wrought-iron balcony, art deco furniture, a vaulted ceiling, and a clientele to match: most are young, cell phone–carrying professionals. Café au lait and alcoholic drinks are served all day until closing.

CASSIDY'S (42 Lower Camden St., tel. 01/475–1429) is a quiet neighborhood pub with a pint of stout so good that former president Bill Clinton dropped in for one during a visit to Dublin.

CHIEF O'NEILL'S (Smithfield Village, tel. 01/817–3838), a Dublin hotel, has a large bar-café with an open, airy atmosphere and often hosts traditional Irish sessions.

The **COBBLESTONE** (N. King St., tel. 01/872–1799) is a glorious house of ale in the best Dublin tradition. Popular with Smithfield market workers, it has a chatty atmosphere and live music that are attracting a wider crowd.

DAVY BYRNE'S (21 Duke St., tel. 01/671–1298) is a pilgrimage stop for Joyceans. In *Ulysses*, Leopold Bloom stops in here for a glass of burgundy and a Gorgonzola cheese sandwich. He then leaves the pub and walks to Dawson Street, where he helps a blind man cross the road. Unfortunately, the pub is unrecognizable from Joyce's day, but it still serves some fine pub grub.

DOCKERS (5 Sir John Rogerson's Quay, tel. 01/677–1692) is a trendy quayside spot east of city center, just around the corner from Windmill Lane Studios, where U2 and other noted bands record; at night the area is a little dicey, so come during the day.

DOHENY & NESBITT (5 Lower Baggot St., tel. 01/676–2945), a traditional spot with snugs, dark wooden decor, and smoke-darkened ceilings, has hardly changed over the decades.

DOYLE'S (9 College St., tel. 01/671–0616), a small, cozy pub, is a favorite with journalists from the *Irish Times*, just across the street.

The **GLOBE** (11 S. Great George's St., tel. 01/671–1220), one of the hippest café-bars in town, draws arty, trendy Dubliners who sip espresso drinks by day and pack the place at night. There's live jazz on Sunday.

GROGANS (15 S. William St., tel. 01/677–9320), also known as the Castle Lounge, is a small place packed with creative folk.

GUBU (Capel St., tel. 01/874–0710) is the newest venture north of the river by the owners of the hugely successful Globe. The pool table downstairs is a bonus.

HOGAN'S (35 Great St. George's St., tel. 01/6677–5904), a huge floor space on two levels, is jammed on most nights, but the old place maintains its style through it all and the beer is top shelf.

HORSESHOE BAR (Shelbourne Méridien Hotel, 27 St. Stephen's Green, tel. 01/676–6471) is a popular meeting place for Dublin's

dublin pubs

businesspeople and politicians, though it has comparatively little space for drinkers around the semicircular bar.

KEHOE'S (9 S. Anne St., tel. 01/677–8312) is popular with Trinity students and academics. The tiny back room is cozy.

MCDAID'S (3 Harry St., tel. 01/679–4395) attracted boisterous Brendan Behan and other leading writers in the 1950s; its wild literary reputation still lingers, although the bar has been discreetly modernized and the atmosphere is altogether quieter.

MOTHER REDCAP'S TAVERN (Back La., tel. 01/453–8306) is an authentic re-creation of a 17th-century Dublin tavern, with stone walls from an old flour mill, beams, and old prints of the city.

MODERN GREEN BAR (31 Wexford St., tel. 01/470–0583) mixes some of Dublin's top DJs with a wide selection of imported beers. The result: a young, hip crowd that likes to dance.

MULLIGAN'S (8 Poolbeg St., tel. 01/677–5582) is synonymous in Dublin with a truly inspirational pint of Guinness. Until a few years ago no women were admitted. Today journalists, locals, and students of both genders flock here for the perfect pint.

NEARY'S (1 Chatham St., tel. 01/677–7371), which has an exotic Victorian-style interior, was once the haunt of music-hall artists, as well as that of a certain literary set including Brendan Behan. Join the actors from the adjacent Gaiety Theatre for a good pub lunch.

O'DONOGHUE'S (15 Merrion Row, tel. 01/676–2807), a cheerful, smoky hangout, has impromptu musical performances that often spill out onto the street.

RYAN'S PUB (28 Parkgate St., tel. 01/677–6097) is one of Dublin's last genuine, late-Victorian-era pubs and has changed little since its last (1896) remodeling.

STAG'S HEAD (1 Dame Ct., tel. 01/679–3701) dates from 1770 and was rebuilt in 1895; theater people from the nearby Olympia, journalists, and Trinity students turn up around the unusual counter, fashioned from Connemara red marble.

TONER'S (139 Lower Baggot St., tel. 01/676–3090), though billed as a Victorian bar, actually goes back 200 years, with an original flagstone floor to prove its antiquity, as well as wooden drawers running up to the ceiling, a relic of the days when bars doubled as grocery shops. Oliver St. John Gogarty accompanied W. B. Yeats here, in what was purportedly the latter's only visit to a pub.

COUNTY DUBLIN—SOUTHSIDE

JOHNNIE FOX'S (Glencullen, Co. Dublin, tel. 01/295–5647), 12 km (8 mi) from the city center, sits 1,000 ft up in the Dublin Mountains, making it the highest licensed premises in Ireland. It's approached by a winding and steeply climbing road that turns off the main Dublin–Enniskerry road at Stepaside. Steadfastly refusing to bow to the whims of modernization, it has maintained all of its traditional character—oak tables, rough-stone floor flags strewn with sawdust, and ancient bric-a-brac, including copper kettles, crockery, old prints, and guns—appearing very much as it did in the early 19th century, when Daniel O'Connell used it as a safe house for his seditious meetings. Lunch and dinner are served; the specialty is seafood, which is alone worth the journey. In the evenings there is traditional Irish music.

TEMPLE BAR

The **FRONT LOUNGE** (33 Parliament St., Temple Bar, tel. 01/679–3988), a modern pub, caters to a mixed crowd of young professionals, both gay and straight.

OLIVER ST. JOHN GOGARTY (57 Fleet St., Temple Bar, tel. 01/671–1822) is a lively bar that attracts all ages and nationalities and overflows in summer. On most nights there is traditional Irish music upstairs.

PALACE BAR (21 Fleet St., Temple Bar, tel. 01/677–9290), scarcely changed over the past 60 years, is tiled and rather barren looking but popular with journalists and writers (the Irish Times is nearby). The walls are hung with cartoons drawn by the illustrators who used to spend time here.

Gay and Lesbian Pubs

The **GEORGE** (89 S. Great George's St., tel. 01/478–2983), Dublin's two-floor main gay pub, draws an almost entirely male crowd; its nightclub stays open until 2:30 AM nightly except Tuesday. The "alternative bingo night," with star drag act Miss Shirley Temple Bar, is a riot of risqué fun.

OUT ON THE LIFFEY (27 Ormond Quay, tel. 01/872–2480) is Dublin's second gay pub; it draws a mixed crowd of men and women.

Irish Cabaret

BALLSBRIDGE/SOUTH CITY CENTER
DOYLE BURLINGTON HOTEL (Upper Leeson St., tel. 01/660–5222) has a high-class lounge featuring a well-performed Irish cabaret, with dancing, music, and song.

JURYS HOTEL (Pembroke Rd., Ballsbridge, tel. 01/660–5000) stages a cabaret show similar to that at the Doyle Burlington hotel.

CITY CENTER
CASTLE INN (Christ Church Pl., tel. 01/475–1122) is really just a huge pub that has traditional Irish music and dancing with dinner in a medieval-style banquet hall.

COUNTY DUBLIN—NORTHSIDE

ABBEY TAVERN (Howth, tel. 01/839–0307) has a rip-roaring cabaret with rousing traditional Irish songs.

CLONTARF CASTLE (Castle Ave., Clontarf, tel. 01/833–2321) offers a spectacular setting for a traditional night of song and comedy.

Irish Music and Dancing

SOUTH DUBLIN

COMHALTAS CEOLTÓIRI ÉIREANN (35 Belgrave Sq., Monkstown, tel. 01/280–0295) has boisterous summer evenings of genuine Irish music and dancing.

HARCOURT HOTEL (Harcourt St., tel. 01/478–3677) is where some of the best traditional musicians gather for wild jam sessions.

Nightclubs

The dominant sound in Dublin's nightclubs is electronic dance music, and the crowd that flocks to the clubs every night of the week is of the trendy, under-25 generation. However, there are a couple of clubs where you're more likely to hear tango than techno, such as the weekend nightclub at the Gaiety Theatre, Thursday night at the Pod, and Sunday night at Lillie's Bordello. **VELURE** (tel. 01/670–3750) is one of Dublin's most successful nightclub promoters, organizing live music, DJs, and theme parties; call to find out what's going on.

CITY CENTER

LEESON STREET—just off St. Stephen's Green and known as "the strip"—is a main nightclub area from pub closing time to 4 AM, although it has lost its gloss in recent years with the arrival of a number of lap-dancing establishments. The dress code at Leeson Street's dance clubs is informal, but jeans and sneakers are not welcome. Most of these clubs are licensed only to sell wine, and the prices can be exorbitant (up to €26 for a mediocre bottle); the upside is that most don't charge to get in.

LILLIE'S BORDELLO (Grafton St., tel. 01/679–9204) is a popular spot for a trendy, professional crowd, as well as for rock and film stars. On Sunday night, the strict dress code is relaxed for a night of live music and DJs.

The **POD** (Harcourt St., tel. 01/478–0166), also known as the "Place of Dance," is Dublin's most-renowned dance club, especially among the younger set. Entry is judged as much on clothing as on age; it helps to look either stylish or rich, except on Thursday night, when the club hosts a no-frills, no-nonsense night of dance-floor jazz and funk.

The **RED BOX** (Old Harcourt St. Station, Harcourt St., tel. 01/478–0166), adjacent to the Pod and the Chocolate Bar, can pack in more than 1,000 people and surround them with state-of-the-art sound and light. It regularly hosts Irish and international rock acts as well as celebrity DJs from Europe and the United States. As do most other Dublin rock venues, the Red Box has full bar facilities.

RENARDS (St. Fredrick St., tel. 01/677–5876) is a club for thirtysomethings who like to let their hair down. The music can be a bit predictable, but the jazz and supper club is a better option.

RÍ RA (Dame Ct., tel. 01/677–4835) is part of the hugely popular Globe bar. The name means "uproar" in Irish, and on most nights the place does go a little wild. It's one of the best spots in Dublin for no-frills, fun dancing. Upstairs is more low-key.

TEMPLE BAR
The **KITCHEN** (E. Essex St., tel. 01/677–6359) is in the basement of the Clarence hotel; its popularity, mainly with an under-30 crowd, owes much to its owners, Bono and the Edge of U2.

THE ARTS

Theater and popular music are the dominant performing arts in Dublin but by no means the only ones; they are supplemented by a handful of cinemas, an opera company, classical music, art galleries, and the city's vibrant pub life.

Art Galleries

THE BRIDGE. This restored 18th-century Georgian house on the river has been turned into an impressive, open-plan gallery. An internal bridge leads from the gallery shop to a big space at the back which houses exhibits of established and rising Irish artists in all media. *6 Upper Ormond Quay, tel. 01/872–9702. Mon.–Sat. 10–6, Sun. 2–5.*

GREEN ON RED GALLERIES. This rather unprepossessing gallery, near the back of Trinity College, is one of Dublin's best, with constantly changing exhibitions featuring the work of some of the country's—and Britain's—most promising up-and-coming artists. *26–28 Lombard St. E, tel. 01/671–3414. Weekdays 11–6, Sat. 11–5.*

KERLIN GALLERY. Perhaps Dublin's most important commercial gallery, this large space behind Grafton Street exhibits the work of many of Ireland's most important contemporary artists, including such internationally recognized figures as New York–based Sean Scully, Kathy Prendergast, Paul Seawright, and Stephen McKenna. *Anne's La., S. Anne St., tel. 01/670–9093. Weekdays 10–5:45, Sat. 11–4:30.*

NATIONAL PHOTOGRAPHIC ARCHIVE. A real treasure trove of Irish photographs from the late 19th and early 20th centuries, the Archive also hosts exhibits of work from contemporary Irish photographers, North and South. *Temple Bar, tel. 01/603–0200. Weekdays 10–5, Sat. 10–2.*

ORIGINAL PRINT GALLERY. An ultramodern building by the same prominent Dublin architect who designed Temple Bar Gallery, this place specializes in handmade limited editions of prints by Irish artists. Also in the building, the **Black Church Print Studio** (tel. 01/677–3629) exhibits prints. 4 Temple Bar, tel. 01/677–3657. Tues.–Fri. 10:30–5:30, Sat. 11–5, Sun. 2–6.

RUBICON GALLERY. This second-floor gallery overlooking St. Stephen's Green holds a number of yearly exhibitions featuring work in all media from sculpture to photography. 10 St. Stephen's Green, tel. 01/670–8055. Mon.–Sat. 11–5:30.

SOLOMON GALLERY. Not exactly a risk taker, the Solomon has slowly developed a name as one of Dublin's leading fine-art galleries. Powerscourt Townhouse Centre, S. William St., tel. 01/679–4237. Mon.–Sat. 10–5:30.

TEMPLE BAR GALLERY. A flagship of the Temple Bar redevelopment project, this gallery exhibits the work of emerging Irish photographers, painters, sculptors, and other artists in rotating monthly shows. 5–9 Temple Bar, tel. 01/671–0073. Mon.–Sat. 11–6, Sun. 2–6.

Classical Music and Opera

The **BANK OF IRELAND ARTS CENTER** (Foster Pl. S, tel. 01/671–1488) is the perfect sport for a regular lunchtime recital.

NATIONAL CONCERT HALL (Earlsfort Terr., tel. 01/475–1666), just off St. Stephen's Green, is Dublin's main theater for classical music of all kinds, from symphonies to chamber groups. It's also home to the National Symphony Orchestra of Ireland.

OPERA IRELAND (John Player House, 276–288 S. Circular Rd., tel. 01/453–5519) performs at the Gaiety Theatre; call to find out what's on and when.

OPERA THEATRE COMPANY (18 St. Andrew St., tel. 01/679–4962) is Ireland's only touring opera company, performing at venues in Dublin and throughout the country.

ROYAL HOSPITAL KILMAINHAM (Military Rd., tel. 01/671–8666) presents frequent classical concerts in its magnificent historic interior.

ST. STEPHEN'S CHURCH (Merrion Sq., tel. 01/288–0663) has a regular program of choral and orchestral events in its glorious setting.

Film

Dublin has two dozen cinema screens in the city center and a number of large, multiscreen cinema complexes in the suburbs, showing current releases made in Ireland and abroad.

IRISH FILM CENTRE (6 Eustace St., tel. 01/677–8788) shows classic and new independent films.

SAVOY CINEMA (O'Connell St., tel. 01/874–6000), just across from the General Post Office, is a four-screen theater with the largest screen in the country.

SCREEN CINEMA (2 Townsend St., tel. 01/671–4988), between Trinity College and the O'Connell Street Bridge, is a popular three-screen art-house cinema.

UGC MULTIPLEX (Parnell Center, Parnell St., tel. 01/872–8400), a 12-screen theater just off O'Connell Street, is the city center's only multiplex movie house and shows the latest commercial features.

Jazz

JJ SMYTH'S (12 Aungier St., tel. 01/475–2565) is an old-time jazz venue where Louis Stewart, the granddaddy of Irish jazz, has a regular slot.

JURYS BALLSBRIDGE (Pembroke Rd., Ballsbridge, tel. 01/660–5000) attracts the country's top jazz musicians and voices to its lively Sunday sessions.

PENDULUM CLUB (The Norseman, at Eustace and E. Essex Sts., Temple Bar, tel. 01/671–5135) is the place to go for good jazz, with some of Ireland's top acts featured as well as guest appearances by internationally recognized musicians.

Rock and Contemporary Music

HQ (57 Middle Abbey St., tel. 01/889–9403) is a very comfortable 500-seater venue, at the Hot Press Irish Music Hall of Fame. It has a balcony and restaurant and attracts international big-name acts.

The **INTERNATIONAL BAR** (Wicklow St., tel. 01/677–9250) has a long-established, tiny, get-close-to-the band venue upstairs. It hosts theater in the afternoons.

OLYMPIA THEATRE (72 Dame St., tel. 01/677–7744) puts on its "Midnight from the Olympia" shows every Friday and Saturday from midnight to 2 AM, with everything from rock to country.

The **POINT** (Eastlink Br., tel. 01/836–3633), a 6,000-capacity arena about 1 km (½ mi) east of the Custom House on the Liffey, is Dublin's premier venue for internationally renowned acts. Call or send a self-addressed envelope to receive a list of upcoming shows; tickets can be difficult to obtain, so book early.

TEMPLE BAR MUSIC CENTRE (Curved St., tel. 01/670–0533)—a music venue, rehearsal space, television studio, and pub rolled into one—buzzes with activity every day of the week. Live acts range from rock bands to ethnic music to singer-songwriters.

WHELAN'S (25 Wexford St., tel. 01/478–0766), just off the southeastern corner of St. Stephen's Green, is one of the city's best—and most popular—music venues, featuring well-known acts performing everything from rock to folk to traditional.

Theater

ABBEY THEATRE (Lower Abbey St., tel. 01/878–7222), the home of Ireland's national theater company, stages mainstream, mostly traditional Irish plays. Its sister theater at the same address, the **Peacock,** offers more experimental drama. In 1904 W. B. Yeats and his patron, Lady Gregory, opened the theater, which became a major center for the Irish literary renaissance—the place that first staged works by J. M. Synge and Sean O'Casey, among many others. The original theater burned down in 1951, but it reopened with a modern design in 1966.

ANDREW'S LANE THEATRE (9–11 Andrew's La., tel. 01/679–5720) presents experimental productions.

GAIETY THEATRE (S. King St., tel. 01/677–1717) is the home of Opera Ireland when it's not showing musical comedy, drama, and revues.

GATE THEATRE (Cavendish Row, Parnell Sq., tel. 01/874–4045), an intimate 371-seat theater in a jewel-like Georgian assembly hall, produces the classics and contemporary plays by leading Irish writers.

NEW PROJECT ARTS CENTRE (39 E. Essex St., tel. 01/671–2321) is a theater and performance space right in the center of Temple Bar. Fringe and mainstream theater, contemporary music, and experimental art all have a home here.

OLYMPIA THEATRE (72 Dame St., tel. 01/677–7744) is Dublin's oldest and premier multipurpose theatrical venue. In addition to its high-profile musical performances, it has seasons of comedy, vaudeville, and ballet.

SAMUEL BECKETT CENTRE (Trinity College, tel. 01/608–2266) is home to Trinity's Drama Department as well as visiting groups from around Europe. Dance is often featured.

TIVOLI (135–138 Francis St., tel. 01/454–4472) brings culture to the heart of old working-class Dublin, the Liberties. Lighter, comedy-based shows and the occasional Shakespeare play are favored.

In This Chapter

Updated by Anto Howard

where to stay

"AN ABSOLUTE AVALANCHE OF NEW HOTELS" is how the *Irish Times* characterized Dublin's hotel boom. New lodgings have sprung up in all areas of the city, including the much-talked-about one in Smithfield, and some in Ballsbridge, an inner "suburb" that's a 20-minute walk from the city center. Demand for rooms means that rates are still high at the best hotels by the standards of any major European or North American city (and factoring in the exchange rate means a hotel room can take a substantial bite out of any traveler's budget). Service charges range from 15% in expensive hotels to zero in moderate and inexpensive ones. Be sure to inquire when you make reservations.

Many hotels have a weekend, or "B&B," rate that's often 30%–40% cheaper than the ordinary rate; some hotels also have a midweek special that provides discounts of up to 35%. These rates are available throughout the year but are harder to get in high season. Ask about them when booking a room (they are available only on a prebooked basis), especially if you plan a brief or weekend stay. If you've rented a car and you're not staying at a hotel with secure parking facilities, it's worth considering a location out of the city center, such as Dalkey or Killiney, where the surroundings are more pleasant and you won't have to worry about parking on city streets, which can be difficult.

Dublin has a decent selection of less-expensive accommodations—including many moderately priced hotels with basic but agreeable rooms. As a general rule of thumb, lodgings on the north side of the river tend to be more affordable than those on the south. Many B&Bs, long the mainstay of the economy end of the market, have upgraded their facilities and now provide rooms with private bathrooms or showers, as well as multichannel color televisions and direct-dial telephones, for around €44.45 a night per person. B&Bs tend to be in suburban areas—generally a 15-minute bus ride from the center of the city. This is not in itself a great drawback, and savings can be significant.

CATEGORY	DUBLIN*
$$$$	over £€280
$$$	£€230–€280
$$	€178–€230
$	under €178

*Prices are for two people in a double room, including 12.5% local sales tax and a service charge (often applied in larger hotels).

CITY CENTER (SOUTHSIDE)

$$$$ **CONRAD DUBLIN INTERNATIONAL.** In a seven-story redbrick and smoked-glass building just off St. Stephen's Green, the Conrad, owned by the Hilton Group, is firmly aimed at international business travelers. Rooms are rather cramped and have uninspiring views of the adjacent office buildings, but they are nicely outfitted with natural wood furnishings, painted in sand colors and pastel greens, and have Spanish marble in the bathrooms. A note to light sleepers: the air-conditioning/heating system can be noisy. The hotel has two restaurants: the informal Plurabelle and the plusher Alexandra Room. The main bar, Alfie Byrne's, named in honor of Dublin's lord mayor for most of the 1930s (a renowned teetotaller), attempts to re-create a traditional Irish pub atmosphere. *Earlsfort Terr., Dublin 2, tel. 01/676–5555, fax 01/676–5424, www.conradinternational.ie. 182 rooms with bath, 9 suites. 2 restaurants, bar, in-room data ports, in-room safes, in-room VCRs, minibars, no-smoking floor, no-smoking rooms, room service, gym, concierge, business services, meeting rooms, free parking. AE, DC, MC, V.*

\$\$\$\$ FITZWILLIAM HOTEL. The Fitzwilliam has been dubbed a "designer" hotel for its impeccable decor: everything from light fixtures to luggage racks to staff uniforms is high design. The modern glass building has a large roof garden and overlooks the park. The spacious rooms are furnished in a contemporary, comfortable style. Conrad Gallagher, one of Ireland's young up-and-coming chefs, presides over the rooftop restaurant. *St. Stephen's Green, Dublin 2, tel. 01/478–7000, fax 01/478–7878, www.fitzwilliamh.com. 135 rooms with bath, 2 suites. Restaurant, bar, brasserie, in-room data ports, no-smoking rooms, room service, gym, laundry service, business services, meeting rooms. AE, DC, MC, V.*

\$\$\$\$ MERRION. The home of Arthur Wellesley, the Duke of Wellington
★ and hero of the Battle of Waterloo, is one of the four exactingly restored Georgian town houses that make up this luxurious hotel. The stately rooms are richly appointed in classic Georgian style down to the last detail—from the crisp linen sheets to the Carrara marble bathrooms. Some are vaulted with delicate Adamesque plasterwork ceilings, and others are graced with magnificent, original marble fireplaces. The Garden Wing, at the back of the hotel behind the elegant gardens laid out by Irish landscape designer Jim Reynolds, has smaller rooms than the main house, but they are just as ornate. Leading Dublin restaurateur Patrick Guilbaud has his eponymous restaurant here. *Upper Merrion St., Dublin 2, tel. 01/603–0600, fax 01/603–0700, www.merrionhotel.com. 127 rooms with bath, 18 suites. 2 restaurants, 2 bars, in-room data ports, in-room safes, in-room VCRs, minibars, no-smoking floor, no-smoking rooms, room service, indoor pool, barbershop, hair salon, massage, steam room, dry cleaning, laundry service, concierge, business services, meeting rooms, free parking. AE, DC, MC, V.*

\$\$\$\$ SHELBOURNE MÉRIDIEN HOTEL. Paris has the Ritz, New York has
★ the Plaza, and Dublin has the Shelbourne. The grand old history (Ireland's constitution was signed in Room 112 in 1921) of this grand old place was written by no less than celebrated novelist and wit Elizabeth Bowen. One step past the ornate redbrick and white-gingerbread facade and you know you're in Dublin: Waterford

chandeliers, gleaming old masters on the wall, and Irish Chippendale chairs invite you to linger in the lobby—as many fabled names have done so since this city showplace opened in 1824. Each guest room has fine, carefully selected furniture and luxurious drapes, with splendid antiques in the older rooms. Those in front overlook St. Stephen's Green, but rooms in the back, without a view, are quieter. The restaurant, 27 The Green, is one of the most elegant rooms in Dublin; Lord Mayor's Lounge, off the lobby, is a perfect rendezvous spot and offers a lovely afternoon tea—a real Dublin tradition. *27 St. Stephen's Green, Dublin 2, tel. 01/663–4500; 800/543–4300 in the U.S., fax 01/661–6006, www.shelbourne.ie. 194 rooms with bath, 9 suites. 2 restaurants, 2 bars, indoor pool, hot tub, sauna, health club, free parking. AE, DC, MC, V.*

$$$$ WESTBURY. This comfortable, modern hotel is in the heart of southside Dublin, right off the city's buzzing shopping mecca, Grafton Street. Join elegantly dressed Dubliners for afternoon tea in the spacious mezzanine-level main lobby, furnished with antiques. Alas, the utilitarian rooms—painted in pastels—don't share the lobby's elegance. More inviting are the suites, which combine European decor with tasteful Japanese screens and prints. The flowery Russell Room serves formal lunches and dinners; the downstairs Sandbank, a seafood restaurant and bar, resembles a Joycean-period establishment. *Grafton St., Dublin 2, tel. 01/679–1122, fax 01/679–7078, www.jurysdoyle.com. 203 rooms with bath, 8 suites. 2 restaurants, bar, minibars, no-smoking rooms, room service, dry cleaning, laundry service, free parking. AE, DC, MC, V.*

$$$ DAVENPORT. The gorgeous, bright-yellow neoclassic facade of this hotel, just behind Trinity College, was originally built in the 1860s to front a church. The reasonably spacious rooms and larger suites are fitted in tasteful, deep colors and functional furnishings. The hotel restaurant, Lanyon's, serves breakfast, lunch, and dinner amid traditional Georgian decor. *Merrion Sq., Dublin 2, tel. 01/661–6800; 800/327–0200 in the U.S., fax 01/661–5663, www.ocallaghanhotels.ie. 118 rooms with bath, 2 suites. Restaurant,* bar, in-room VCRs, minibars, no-smoking rooms, room service, dry cleaning, laundry service, concierge, business services, meeting rooms, free parking. AE, DC, MC, V.

$$ CLARION STEPHEN'S HALL HOTEL & SUITES. Dublin's only all-suite hotel is in a tastefully modernized Georgian town house just off Stephen's Green. The suites, considerably larger than the average hotel room, include one or two bedrooms, a separate sitting room, a fully equipped kitchen, and bath. They are comfortably equipped with quality modern furniture. Top-floor suites have spectacular city views, and ground-floor suites have private entrances. Morel's Restaurant serves breakfast, lunch, and dinner. 14–17 Lower Leeson St., Dublin 2, tel. 01/661–0585, fax 01/661–0606, www.premgroup.ie. 34 suites. Restaurant, 2 bars, no-smoking rooms, room service, meeting rooms, free parking. AE, DC, MC, V.

$–$$ CENTRAL HOTEL. Established in 1887, this grand, old-style redbrick hotel is in the heart of the center city, steps from Grafton Street, Temple Bar, and Dublin Castle. Rooms are small but have high ceilings and practical but tasteful furniture. Adjacent to the hotel is Molly Malone's Tavern, a lively hotel bar with plenty of regulars who come for the atmosphere and the live, traditional Irish music on Friday and Saturday nights. The restaurant and Library Bar—one of the best spots in the city for a quiet pint—are on the first floor. 1–5 Exchequer St., Dublin 2, tel. 01/679–7302, fax 01/679–7303, www.centralhotel.ie. 67 rooms with bath, 3 suites. Restaurant, 2 bars, room service, dry cleaning, laundry service, concierge, business services, meeting rooms. AE, DC, MC, V.

$–$$ DRURY COURT HOTEL. This small hotel is a two-minute walk from Grafton Street and just around the corner from some of the city's best restaurants. Rooms are done in subtle greens, golds, and burgundies. The parquet-floored rathskeller dining room serves breakfast and dinner; lunch is served in the casual Digges Lane Bar, frequented by many young Dubliners. 28–30 Lower Stephens St., Dublin 2, tel. 01/475–1988, fax 01/478–5730, indigo.ie/˜druryct/.

30 rooms with bath, 2 suites. Restaurant, bar, room service, dry cleaning, laundry service, meeting room. AE, DC, MC, V.

$ AVALON HOUSE. Many young, independent travelers rate this cleverly restored, Victorian redbrick building the most appealing of Dublin's hostels. A 2-minute walk from Grafton Street and 5–10 minutes from some of the city's best music venues, the hostel has a mix of dormitories, rooms without bath, and rooms with bath. The dorm rooms and en-suite quads all have loft areas that offer more privacy than you'd typically find in a multibed room. The Avalon Café serves food until 10 PM but is open as a common room after hours. 55 Aungier St., Dublin 2, tel. 01/475–0001, fax 01/475–0303, www.avalon-house.ie. 35 4-bed rooms with bath, 5 4-bed rooms without bath, 4 twin rooms with bath, 22 twin rooms without bath, 4 single rooms without bath, 5 12-bed dorms, 1 10-bed dorm, 1 26-bed dorm. Bar, café. AE, MC, V.

$ JURYS CHRISTCHURCH INN. Expect few frills at this functional budget hotel, part of a Jurys minichain that offers a low, fixed room rate for up to three adults or two adults and two children. The **Jurys Custom House Inn** (Custom House Quay, Dublin 1, tel. 01/607–5000, fax 01/829–0400), at the International Financial Services Centre, operates according to the same plan. The biggest plus is the pleasant location, facing Christ Church Cathedral and within walking distance of most city-center attractions. The rather spartan rooms are decorated in pastel colors and utilitarian furniture. Christ Church Pl., Dublin 8, tel. 01/454–0000, fax 01/454–0012, www. jurysdoyle.com. 182 rooms with bath. Restaurant, bar, no-smoking rooms, parking (fee). AE, DC, MC, V.

$ KILRONAN HOUSE. A five-minute walk from St. Stephen's Green,
★ this is a large, late-19th-century terraced house, with a white facade that has been carefully converted. The furnishings are updated each year. Richly patterned wallpaper and carpets grace guest rooms. Orthopedic beds (rather rare in Dublin hotels, let alone guest houses) help to guarantee a restful night's sleep. 70

Adelaide Rd., Dublin 2, tel. 01/475–5266, fax 01/478–2841, www. dublinn.com. 15 rooms with bath. Free parking. MC, V.

$ NUMBER 31. Two Georgian mews strikingly renovated in the early '60s as the private home of Sam Stephenson, Ireland's leading modern architect, are now connected via a small garden to the grand town house they once served. Together they form a marvelous guest house a short walk from St. Stephen's Green. Owners Deirdre and Noel Comer serve made-to-order breakfasts at refectory tables in the balcony dining room. The white-tiled sunken living room, with its black leather sectional sofa and modern artwork that includes a David Hockney print, will make you think you're in California, not Dublin. *31 Leeson Close, Dublin 2, tel. 01/676–5011, fax 01/676–2929, www.number31.ie. 18 rooms with bath. No-smoking rooms, dry cleaning, laundry service, free parking. AE, MC, V.*

TEMPLE BAR

$$–$$$ THE CLARENCE. You might well bump into celebrity friends of co-owners Bono and the Edge of U2 at this contemporary hotel, understated to the point of austerity. Stone floors, unadorned oak wainscoting, and a leather-lined elevator set the slightly chaotic tone downstairs, where the Octagon Bar and the Tea Room Restaurant are popular Temple Bar watering holes. Guest rooms are done in a mishmash of earth tones accented with deep purple, gold, cardinal red, and royal blue. With the exception of those in the penthouse suite, rooms are small; but *very* comfortable beds, sparkling bathrooms, and views of the Liffey, from the front rooms, compensate. The laissez-faire service seems to take its cue from the minimalist decor, so if you like to be pampered, stay elsewhere. *6–8 Wellington Quay, Dublin 2, tel. 01/407–0800, fax 01/407–0820, www.theclarence.ie. 46 rooms with bath, 4 suites. Restaurant, bar, minibars, no-smoking rooms, dry cleaning, laundry service, meeting rooms, free parking. AE, DC, MC, V.*

$–$$ ARLINGTON HOTEL. A converted auction house on the quays is the setting for this privately owned boutique hotel. Pass between the gold lions guarding the door and enter a medieval great hall with suits of armor, sumptuous swags, and creaky floors. The theme continues in the bar; boisterous and echo-filled, it's more mead hall than cozy pub. Rich upholstery, romantic lighting, and hearty Irish fare (full breakfast is included in the rate) make the restaurant more intimate. Upstairs the corridors and rooms have a Georgian feel, with soothing pastel yellow or lavender walls; spreads and drapes are awash in golds, rusts, and blues and have patterns and details evocative of tapestries. The hotel also has limited off-street parking, though your way might be blocked by a Guinness truck. *23–25 Bachelor's Walk, O'Connell Bridge, Dublin 1, tel. 01/804–9100, fax 01/804–9112, www.arlington.ie. 115 rooms with bath. Restaurant, bar, in-room data ports, no-smoking rooms, dance club, baby-sitting, laundry service, meeting rooms, free parking. AE, DC, MC, V.*

$–$$ PARLIAMENT. Although the Parliament is in one of Dublin's finest Edwardian buildings, its interior is very much functional, if tidy, and attracts a mostly business clientele. They are drawn by the location near the Central Bank and a few blocks down from Trinity College. Rooms are a good size, with a simple, slightly monotonous beige and off-white scheme. The Senate Restaurant and Forum Bar keep up the democratic theme. *Lord Edward St., Dublin 2, tel. 01/670–8777, fax 01/670–8787, www.regencyhotels.com. 63 rooms with bath. Restaurant, bar, no-smoking rooms. AE, DC, MC, V.*

$–$$ TEMPLE BAR. In a former bank building just around the corner from Trinity College, this hotel has an Art Deco lobby with a large and old-fashioned cast-iron fireplace, natural-wood furniture, and lots of plants. Off the lobby are a small cocktail bar and the bright, open, glass-roofed Terrace Restaurant, which serves sandwiches, pastas, omelets, and fish all day. Mahogany furnishings and autumn green and rust colors adorn guest rooms, nearly all of which have double beds, making them more than a little cramped. The Boomerang nightclub on the premises is open to both guests and the public. *Fleet St., Dublin 2, tel. 01/677–3333, fax 01/677–3088, www.tarahotelgroup.ie. 133 rooms with bath, 2 suites. Restaurant, 2 bars, nightclub, parking (fee). AE, DC, MC, V.*

$ **PARAMOUNT.** On the corner of Parliament Street and Essex Gate at the heart of Temple Bar, this medium-size hotel has opted to maintain its classy Victorian facade. Built only 30 yards from the River Liffey, the exterior is full of interesting, organic curves. Lead-lined glass and stained wood give the front windows an authoritative touch, as if the Paramount intends to be around for quite some time. The foyer continues this theme of solid elegance, with ridiculously comfortable leather couches, bleached-blond oak floors, and Burgundy red curtains. The bedrooms are all dark woods and subtle colors, very 1930s; you just know if Bogart and Bacall ever came to Dublin they'd have to stay here. *Parliament St. and Essex Gate, Dublin 2, tel. 01/417–9900, fax 01/417–9904, www.paramounthotel.ie. 70 rooms with bath. Restaurant, bar, in-room data ports, no-smoking rooms, laundry service. AE, DC, MC, V.*

SOUTH CITY CENTER—BALLSBRIDGE

$$$$ **BERKELEY COURT.** The most quietly elegant of Dublin's large modern hotels, Berkeley Court has a glass-and-concrete exterior designed in a modern, blocklike style set in verdant grounds. Inside, the vast white-tiled and plushly carpeted lobby has roomy sofas and antique planters. The large rooms are decorated in golds, yellows, and greens, with antiques or reproductions of period furniture; bathrooms are tiled in marble. The five luxury suites have hot tubs. The Berkeley Room restaurant has table d'hôte and à la carte menus; the more informal Conservatory Grill, with large windows, serves grilled food and snacks. *Lansdowne Rd., Dublin 4, tel. 01/660–1711; 800/550–0000 in the U.S., fax 01/661–7238, www.jurysdoyle.com. 159 rooms with bath, 29 suites. 2 restaurants, bar, no-smoking rooms, room service, barbershop, hair salon, gym, shops, dry cleaning, laundry service, business services, meeting rooms, free parking. AE, DC, MC, V.*

$$$$ FOUR SEASONS. The brash, postmodern architecture of this hotel has been the subject of much controversy. One national newspaper claimed the Californian architect thought he was building for Beverly Hills, not Ballsbridge. His creation is a six-floor mix of Victorian and Georgian design with modern glass and concrete construction. The giant luxury accommodation is ideally situated, at the center of a desirable residential enclave. Its impressive landscaping lends it the air of an oasis in the city, and a big effort has been made to ensure a bit of greenery is on view from most rooms. Rooms are spacious, with large windows that allow the light to flood in. *Simmonscourt Rd., Dublin 4, tel. 01/665–4000, fax 01/665–4099, www.fourseasons.com. 192 rooms with bath, 67 suites. Restaurant, bar, coffee shop, indoor pool, hot tub, shop, dry cleaning, laundry service, business services, meeting rooms, free parking. AE, DC, MC, V.*

$$$$ HERBERT PARK HOTEL. The Herbert Park sits adjacent to a park of the same name and beside the River Dodder. The large lobby has floor-to-ceiling windows and a slanted glass roof. The spacious bar, terrace lounge, and restaurant are Japanese-inspired. Relaxing shades of blue and cream predominate in the nicely sized rooms; all have individually controlled air-conditioning, a large desk, and two telephone lines. Some look onto the park. Two of the suites have large balconies with views of the park or the leafy suburbs. The restaurant has a terrace where you can dine in warm weather. *Ballsbridge, Dublin 4, tel. 01/667–2200, fax 01/667–2595, www.herbertparkhotel.ie. 150 rooms with bath, 3 suites. Restaurant, bar, gym, business services, free parking. AE, DC, MC, V.*

$$$–$$$$ JURYS BALLSBRIDGE AND THE TOWERS. These adjoining seven-story hotels, a short cab ride from the center of town, are popular with businesspeople and vacationers. They have more atmosphere than most comparable modern hotels, though the Towers has an edge over Jurys Ballsbridge, its older (it dates from 1962), larger, less-expensive companion. Jurys Ballsbridge has large, plainly decorated rooms with light walls and brown drapes; furnishings are functional but uninspired. The Towers' rooms are a third larger than those of Jurys, decorated in blue and gold with built-in, natural-wood furniture; the large beds and armchairs are comfortable. All the suites in both hotels have their own sitting rooms and kitchenettes. The Dubliner pub in Jurys Ballsbridge is modeled on an old country kitchen; it is popular with upwardly mobile locals and guests. *Jurys Ballsbridge: Pembroke Rd.; The Towers: Lansdowne Rd., Ballsbridge, Dublin 4, tel. 01/660–5000, fax 01/679–7078, jurysdoyle.com. Jurys Ballsbridge: 300 rooms with bath, 3 suites; the Towers: 100 rooms with bath, 4 suites. 2 restaurants, bar, coffee shop, indoor-outdoor pool, hot tub, shop, cabaret (May–Oct.), dry cleaning, laundry service, business services, meeting rooms, free parking. AE, DC, MC, V.*

$$$ DOYLE BURLINGTON. Dublin's largest hotel is about five minutes by car from the city center. Public rooms, especially the large bar, have mahogany counters and hanging plants that enhance the conservatory-style setting. The generous-size rooms, in the usual modern, plush neutral tones, have large picture windows. At night, Annabel's nightclub and the seasonal Irish cabaret are both lively spots. Although the Burlington has no sports and health facilities, the Doyle hotel group has an arrangement that allows you to use the RiverView Sports Club in nearby Clonskeagh for €6.35 a visit. *Upper Leeson St., Dublin 4, tel. 01/660–5222, fax 01/660–8496, www.jurysdoyle.com. 523 rooms with bath. 2 restaurants, 3 bars, room service, shops, cabaret (May–Oct.), nightclub, dry cleaning, laundry service, business service, meeting rooms, free parking. AE, DC, MC, V.*

$$–$$$ HIBERNIAN. Only a 15-minute walk from the city center, this
★ early 20th-century Edwardian nurses' home is now a small luxury hotel. One of the city's most elegant and intimate hostelries, it has retained the distinctive red-and-amber brick facade and has smallish rooms, nicely done in pastels, with deep-pile carpets and comfortable furniture. The public rooms, in cheerful chintz and stripes, include a period-style library and a sun lounge—both

Poolbeg St.
Tara Stati
Ormond Quay
Grattan Br.
River Liffey
Liffey St.
Aston Quay
Fleet St.
Doller St.
Townsend St.
Westmoreland St.
Pearse St.
College St.
Merchant's Quay
Wood Quay
Essex Quay
Fishamble St.
Winetavern St.
Cook St.
Wellington Quay
Temple Bar
Fownes St.
Cope St.
Anglesea St.
College Green
High St.
St. Nicho las St.
Lord Edward
Castle St.
Dame St.
Suffolk St.
Nassau St.
Trinity College
City Hall
Castle
Exchequer St.
Wicklow St.
St. Great George's St.
Ship St. Great
Drury St.
S. William St.
Clarendon St.
Grafton St.
Duke St.
Anne St.
Frederick St.
Molesworth St.
Leinster
Werburgh St.
Golden La.
Dawson St.
Kildare St.
St. Francis St.
Patrick St.
St. Patrick's Park
St. Pat.'s Close
Bride St.
Aungier St.
York St.
St. Stephen's Green W.
St. Stephen's Green N.
Merrion Row
The Coombe
New Row
New Bride St.
Lower Kevin St.
Mercer St.
Cliffe St.
ST. STEPHEN'S GREEN
St. Stephen's Green S.
St. Stephen's Green E.
Lower Clanbrassil St.
Heytesbury St.
Camden St.
Camden Row
Pleasants St.
Harcourt St.
Earlsfort Ter.
Lower Hatch St.
Upper Hatch St.
Lower Leeson St.
Pembroke St.
S. Circular Rd.
Harrington St.
Charlotte St.
Harcourt Rd.
Adelaide Rd.

0   1/4 mi
0   1/2 km

N

Ariel Guest House, 36	Charleville Lodge, 4	Doyle Burlington, 28	Four Seasons, 31
Arlington Hotel, 7	Chief O'Neill's, 5	Drury Court Hotel, 18	Globetrotters Tourist Hotel, 26
Avalon House, 16	The Clarence, 10	Fitzpatrick Castle Dublin, 38	Great Southern Hotel, 3
Berkeley Court, 34	Clarion Stephen's Hall Hotel & Suites, 22	Fitzwilliam Hotel, 19	Herbert Park Hotel, 32
Bewleys at Newlands Cross, 15	Conrad Dublin International, 21	Forte Posthouse, 2	Hibernian, 29
Central Hotel, 13	Davenport, 27		Jurys Ballsbridge and the Towers, 33

Map labels:
Tara St. Station
Gloucester St.
City Quay
Sir John Rogerson's Quay
KEY
DART Railway Station
26
St.
Lombard St. E.
Magennis Pl.
Cardiff's La.
Hanover Quay
Pearse Station
Westland Row
Pearse St.
Macken St.
Ringsend Rd.
Lincoln Place
Clare St.
ester
27
Fenian St.
Hogan Pl.
Lower Grand Canal St.
South Lotts Rd.
Merrion Sq. N.
Merrion Square
Upper Merrion Sq.
Merrion St. West
Merrion Sq. S.
Upper Mount St.
Upper Grand Canal St.
25
Fitzwilliam Ln.
Lower Mount St.
Shelbourne Rd.
Pembroke St.
Lower Fitzwilliam St.
Upper Fitzwilliam St.
Baggot St.
Herbert St.
Herbert Pl.
Grand Canal
North Umberland Rd.
35
36
Lad La.
Haddington Rd.
24
Wilton Terrace
28
29
Upper Baggot St.
31 32
34
Lansdowne Rd.
37 38 39
30
Pembroke Rd.
33
n St.

Jurys Christchurch Inn, 14
Jurys Skylon, 1
Jurys Tara, 37
Kilronan House, 23
Lansdowne, 30
Merrion, 25
The Morrison, 6

Mount Herbert Hotel, 35
Number 31, 24
Paramount, 11
Parliament, 12
Royal Dublin Hotel, 9
Royal Marine, 39

Shelbourne Méridien Hotel, 20
Temple Bar, 8
Westbury, 17

comfortable spaces to relax before or after a dinner in the hotel's intimate restaurant, the Patrick Kavanagh Room. Amid all this Victorian elegance, the owners haven't forgotten the warming touches. *Eastmoreland Pl. off Upper Baggot St., Dublin 4, tel. 01/668–7666 or 800/414243, fax 01/660–2655, hibernianhotel.com. 40 rooms with bath. Restaurant, bar, parking (fee). AE, DC, MC, V.*

$$ LANSDOWNE. This small Ballsbridge hotel has cozy rooms in
★ Georgian style with floral-pattern decor. Photos of sports personalities hang on the walls of the Green Blazer bar in the basement, a popular haunt for local businesspeople and fans of the international rugby matches held at nearby Lansdowne Road; you can get a bite to eat here all day. Next to the bar is Parker's Restaurant, which specializes in seafood and grilled steaks. *27 Pembroke Rd., Dublin 4, tel. 01/668–2522, fax 01/668–5585, www.lansdownehotel.com. 38 rooms with bath, 2 suites. Restaurant, bar, free parking. AE, DC, MC, V.*

$ ARIEL GUEST HOUSE. This redbrick 1850 Victorian guest house
★ in a tree-lined suburb is one of Dublin's finest, just a few steps from a DART stop and a 15-minute walk from St. Stephen's Green. Restored rooms in the main house are lovingly decorated with Victorian and Georgian antiques, Victoriana, and period wallpaper and drapes. The 13 rooms at the back of the house are more spartan, but all are immaculate. A Waterford-crystal chandelier hangs over the comfortable leather and mahogany furniture in the gracious, fireplace-warmed drawing room. Owner Michael O'Brien is an extraordinarily helpful and gracious host. *52 Lansdowne Rd., Dublin 4, tel. 01/668–5512, fax 01/668–5845, www.ariel-house.com. 40 rooms with bath. Breakfast room, free parking. MC, V.*

$ MOUNT HERBERT HOTEL. The Loughran family's sprawling accommodation is made up of a number of large Victorian-era houses. It overlooks some of Ballsbridge's fine rear gardens and is right near the main rugby stadium; the nearby DART will have you in the city center in seven minutes. The simple rooms are painted in light shades and contain little besides beds, but all have bathrooms and 10-channel TVs. You can relax in the lounge; the large restaurant, overlooking the English-style back garden (floodlit at night) and children's play area, serves three meals a day, with unpretentious dinners of steaks and stews. *7 Herbert Rd., Dublin 4, tel. 01/668–4321, fax 01/660–7077, mountherberthotel.ie. 200 rooms with bath. Restaurant, bar, sauna, shop, business services, meeting rooms, free parking. AE, DC, MC, V.*

CITY CENTER (NORTHSIDE)

$$$$ **THE MORRISON.** Halfway between the Ha'penny and Capel Street bridges, it's no more than 10 minutes from Trinity College. The highly modern interior—designed by John Rocha, Ireland's most acclaimed fashion designer—can be a bit cold. He had the last word on everything down to the toiletries and staff uniforms. Rooms are standard in decor but high-tech, with top-of-the-line entertainment units, satellite TV, and ISDN lines. The Halo restaurant has an Asian theme. *Ormond Quay, Dublin 1, tel. 01/887–2400, fax 01/878–3185, morrisonhotel.ie. 88 rooms with bath, 7 suites. 2 restaurants, 2 bars, in-room data ports, in-room VCRs, minibars, no-smoking rooms, room service, dry cleaning, laundry service, concierge, business services, meeting rooms, free parking. AE, DC, MC, V.*

$$–$$$ **CHIEF O'NEILL'S.** Named after a 19th-century Corkman who became chief of police in Chicago, this hotel dominates Smithfield Village. It is part of the complex that also houses Ceol, the traditional music museum. Like the museum, the hotel has a modern design, with a huge lobby-bar area overlooking a cobbled courtyard. Smallish, high-tech rooms all have ISDN lines and look thoroughly up-to-date with chrome fixtures and minimalist furnishings. Top-floor suites have delightful roof-top gardens with views of the city on both sides of the Liffey. The café-bar has live traditional music and contemporary Irish food, and Asian cuisine is available at Kelly & Ping, a bright, airy restaurant off Duck Lane, an integral shopping arcade. *Smithfield Village, Dublin 7, tel. 01/817–3838, fax 01/817–3839, chiefoneills.com. 70 rooms with bath, 3 suites. Restaurant, bar, in-room data ports, in-room VCRs,* minibars, no-smoking rooms, room service, gym, shops, dry cleaning, laundry service, free parking. AE, DC, MC, V.

\$\$ ROYAL DUBLIN HOTEL. O'Connell Street is not what it once was, but this renovated quality hotel has just about a perfect location at the top of the old thoroughfare. All of the northside's major attractions are nearby, and you can walk south to Trinity College in 10 minutes. The public spaces are all well-lit glass and brass, rooms are spacious, and the hotel has a reputation for extra-friendly service. The Georgian Room and Raffles bar try to put on posh English airs, but the casual warmth of the Irish manages to heat up the slightly stuffy atmosphere. *O'Connell St., Dublin 1, tel. 01/873–3666, fax 01/873–3120, royaldublin.com. 117 rooms with bath, 3 suites. Restaurant, bar, in-room data ports, in-room VCRs, minibars, no-smoking rooms, room service, dry cleaning, laundry service. AE, MC, V.*

\$ CHARLEVILLE LODGE. It's worth the short commute to the city center (the No. 10 bus takes five minutes and it's a great walk in good weather) to enjoy the luxury of the great-value Charleville Lodge. The Lodge is part of a row of beautifully restored Victorian terraced houses in the historic Phibsborough area of Dublin's northside. The dramatically lit residents lounge with a working fireplace is the perfect spot to chat with other travelers who have dared to stray off the beaten path. Rooms are brightly colored and spacious. *268–272 N. Circular Rd., Dublin 7, tel. 01/838–6633, fax 01/838–5854, www.charlevillelodge.ie. 30 rooms with bath. Free parking. MC, V.*

\$ GLOBETROTTERS TOURIST HOSTEL. Globetrotters is a giant step up from many Dublin hostels, with a pleasant outdoor courtyard; clean, locking dorm rooms with en-suite showers; a turf fire; comfortable bunk beds (with lamps for late-night reading); and a delicious all-you-can-eat breakfast. Plus, you're within walking distance of the city center, one block from the bus station, and two blocks from the train station. It also owns the Town

House, a cute bed-and-breakfast in the same building. *46 Lower Gardiner St., Dublin 1, tel. 01/873–5893, www.townhouse.ie. 94 dorm beds, 38 double rooms with bath. Restaurant. MC, V.*

SOUTH COUNTY DUBLIN SUBURBS

$$$ ROYAL MARINE. This 1870 seaside hotel has comfortable, capacious rooms with contemporary decor. The suites, with four-poster beds and sitting rooms, preserve the lofty ceilings of the original building. Ask for a room at the front of the hotel, facing Dun Laoghaire harbor. *Marine Rd., Dun Laoghaire, Co. Dublin, tel. 01/280–1911, fax 01/280–1089, www.ryan-hotel.com. 95 rooms with bath, 8 suites. Restaurant, 2 bars, no-smoking rooms, room service, business services, free parking. AE, DC, MC, V.*

$$–$$$ FITZPATRICK CASTLE DUBLIN. With its sweeping views over Dun
★ Laoghaire and Dublin Bay, the Fitzpatrick is worth the 15-km (9-mi) drive from the city center. The original part of the hotel is an 18th-century stone castle, with a substantial modern addition housing rooms; many are furnished with antiques and four-poster beds and have large bathrooms. The hotel is convenient to golf, horseback riding, and fishing; the fitness facilities include an 82-ft heated pool. The views from Killiney Hill, behind the hotel, are spectacular; the seaside village of Dalkey and Killiney Beach are both within walking distance. *Killiney, Co. Dublin, tel. 01/230–5400, fax 01/230–5466, www.fitzpatricks.com. 113 rooms with bath. Restaurant, bar, indoor pool, sauna, steam room, health club, meeting rooms, free parking. AE, DC, MC, V.*

$ BEWLEYS AT NEWLANDS CROSS. On the southwest outskirts of the city, this 1998 four-story hotel is a good option if you're planning to head out of the city early (especially to points in the Southwest and West) and don't want to deal with morning traffic. The hotel is emulating the formula made popular by Jurys Inns, in which rooms—here each has a double bed, a single bed, and a sofa bed—are a flat rate for up to three adults or two adults and two children. *Newlands Cross, Naas Rd., Dublin 22, tel. 01/464–0140, fax 01/464–0900, bewleyshotels.com. 260 rooms with bath. Café, free parking. AE, MC, V.*

$ **JURYS TARA.** On the main coast road 10–15 minutes from the Dun Laoghaire ferry terminal and 6½ km (4 mi) from the city center, this unpretentious, informal seven-story hotel is also close to the Booterstown Marsh Bird Sanctuary. The best rooms are in the original section and face Dublin Bay; rooms in the addition have slightly more modern decor. The restaurant serves grilled fish, steaks, and omelets. The hotel staff is very personable. *Merrion Rd., Dublin 4, tel. 01/269–4666, fax 01/269–1027, www.jurysdoyle.com. 114 rooms with bath. Restaurant, bar, no-smoking rooms, dry cleaning, laundry service, free parking. AE, DC, MC, V.*

DUBLIN AIRPORT

$ **FORTE POSTHOUSE.** This low-rise redbrick structure with a plain exterior has rooms that are basic but spacious. The Bistro Restaurant serves fish and meat entrées, as well as a selection of vegetarian dishes; Sampans serves Chinese cuisine at dinner only. There's live music in the bar on weekends. Guests have access to a nearby health club. *Dublin Airport, tel. 01/808–0500, fax 01/844–6002, www.posthouse-hotel.com. 249 rooms with bath. 2 restaurants, bar, room service, free parking. AE, DC, MC, V.*

$ **GREAT SOUTHERN HOTEL.** Within the airport complex, near the main terminal, and next to the main road into the city center, this modern five-story hotel is part of one of Ireland's most respected chains. The accommodation itself is spacious and comfortable if a little unexciting, but the service is exceptional. *Dublin Airport, tel. 01/844–6000, fax 01/844–6001, www.dubairport.gsh.ie. 147 rooms with bath. Restaurant, bar, room service, free parking. AE, DC, MC, V.*

$ **JURYS SKYLON.** This modern, five-story hotel with a concrete-and-glass facade is on the main road into Dublin city center from the airport. The generous-size rooms are plainly decorated in cool pastels; double beds and a pair of easy chairs are almost the only furniture. A glass-fronted lobby with a large bar and the Rendezvous Room restaurant dominate the public areas. The cooking is adequate but uninspired, with dishes such as grilled steak, poached cod, and omelets. *Upper Drumcondra Rd., Dublin 9, tel. 01/ 837–9121, fax 01/837–2778, www.jurysdoyle.com. 88 rooms with bath. Restaurant, bar, free parking. AE, DC, MC, V.*

practical information

Air Travel

CARRIERS

From the United Kingdom, five airlines now serve destinations in Ireland: Aer Lingus, Ryanair, City Jet, British Airways, and British Midland Airways. Aer Lingus operates 12 flights from Heathrow and Gatwick airports. British Airways has a regular schedule out of Heathrow. British Midland operates 10 flights to Dublin from Heathrow. Ryanair operates several no-frills, low-price flights from Luton and Stanstead airports. City Jet flies from the very central London City Airport. Ryanair is known for being the cheapest, but this means cutting back on comfort and services.

Three airlines have regularly scheduled flights from the United States to Dublin. Aer Lingus flies direct from New York, Boston, Los Angeles, and Chicago to Dublin and Shannon. Continental flies from New York (Newark Airport) to Dublin. Delta flies from Atlanta to Dublin via New York. There are no direct flights to Dublin from Australia or New Zealand.

➤ **MAJOR CARRIERS: Aer Lingus** (tel. 800/223–6537 in the U.S.; 0845/973–7747 or 020/8899–4747 in the U.K.; 02/9244–2123 in Australia; 09/308–3351 in New Zealand, www.aerlingus.ie). **British Airways** (tel. 0845/773–3377 in the U.K.; 800/626747 in Ireland, www.britishairways.com). **Continental** (tel. 800/523–3273 in the U.S.; 1890/925252 in Ireland, www.continental.com). **Delta** (tel.

800/241–4141 in the U.S.; 01/844–4166 or 01/676–8080 in Ireland, www.delta.com).

➤ **SMALLER CARRIERS: Aer Arann** (tel. 01/814–1058 in Ireland, www.aerarann.ie). **Aer Lingus** (tel. 800/223–6537 in the U.S.; 0845/973–7747 or 020/8899–4747 in the U.K.; 02/9244–2123 in Australia; 09/308–3351 in New Zealand, www.aerlingus.ie). **British Midlands** (tel. 0870/607–0555 in the U.K.; 01/283–8833 in Ireland, www.britishmidland.co.uk). **City Jet** (tel. 01/844–5566). **Ryanair** (tel. 01279/666–200 in the U.K.; 01/844–4411 in Ireland, www. ryanair.com).

Airports & Transfers

Dublin Airport, 10 km (6 mi) north of the city center, serves international and domestic airlines.

➤ **AIRPORT INFORMATION: Dublin Airport** (tel. 01/814–1111, www.aer-rinata.ie).

TRANSFERS

Dublin Bus operates a shuttle service between Dublin Airport and the city center with departures outside the arrivals gateway; pay the driver inside the coach. The single fare is €3.80. Service runs from 6:40 AM to 11 PM, at intervals of about 20 minutes (after 8 PM buses run every hour), to as far as Dublin's main bus station (Busaras), behind the Custom House on the northside. Journey time from the airport to the city center is normally 30 minutes, but it may be longer in heavy traffic. If you have time take a regular bus for €1.45.

A taxi is a quicker alternative than the bus to get from the airport to Dublin center. A line of taxis waits by the arrivals gateway; the fare for the 30-mihute journey to any of the main city-center hotels is about €15.25 to €17.80 plus tip (tips don't have to be large but they are increasingly expected). It's advisable to ask about the fare before leaving the airport.

Bus Travel Around Dublin

Dublin has an extensive network of buses—most of them are green double-deckers. Some bus services run on cross-city routes, including the smaller "Imp" buses, but most buses start in the city center. Buses to the north of the city begin in the Lower Abbey Street–Parnell Street area, while those to the west begin in Middle Abbey Street and in the Aston Quay area. Routes to the southern suburbs begin at Eden Quay and in the College Street area. A number of services are links to DART stations, and another regular bus route connects the two main provincial railway stations, Connolly and Heuston. If the destination board indicates AN LÁR, that means that the bus is going to the city center. Late-night buses run Monday to Saturday, on the hour from midnight to 3 PM; the fare is €3.80.

Museumlink is a new shuttle service linking up the Natural History Museum, National Museum, and Collins Barracks. You can catch it outside any of the three museums.

FARES AND SCHEDULES

Timetables (€3.20) are available from Dublin Bus, staffed weekdays 9–5:30, Saturday 9–1. Fares begin at 55p and are paid to the driver, who will accept inexact fares, but you'll have to go to the central office in Dublin to pick up your change as marked on your ticket. Change transactions and the city's heavy traffic can slow service down considerably.

➤ BUS INFORMATION: Dublin Bus (59 Upper O'Connell St., tel. 01/873–4222).

Bus Travel to & from Dublin

Numerous bus services run between Britain and Dublin, but be ready for long hours on the road and possible delays. All buses to Dublin use the Holyhead–Dublin ferry route. National Express, a consortium of bus companies, has Supabus (as its buses are known) services from all major British cities to Dublin. Slattery's, an Irish company, has services from London, Manchester, Liverpool, Oxford, Birmingham, Leeds, and North Wales to Dublin.

Busaras is Dublin's main bus station, just behind the Custom House on the northside.

➤ **BUS INFORMATION: Busaras** (tel. 01/830–2222). **National Express** (tel. 020/7724–0741 in the U.K., www.nationalexpress. co.uk). **Slattery's** (tel. 020/7482–1604 in the U.K.).

Car Rental

If you are renting a car in the Irish Republic and intend to visit Northern Ireland (or vice versa), make this clear when you get your car, and check that the rental insurance applies when you cross the border.

Renting a car in Ireland is far more expensive than organizing a rental before you leave the United States. Rates in Dublin for an economy car with a manual transmission and unlimited mileage begin at €34.30 a day, €177.75 a week (January–April and November–December 15); €44.45 a day, €222.20 a week (May–June and September–October); and €57.15 a day, €304.75 a week (July–August and December 16–31). This includes the Republic's 12½% tax on car rentals.

➤ **MAJOR AGENCIES: Alamo** (tel. 800/522–9696; 020/8759–6200 in the U.K.; www.alamo.com). **Avis** (tel. 800/331–1084; 800/879–2847 in Canada; 02/9353–9000 in Australia; 09/525–1982 in New Zealand; 0870/606–0100 in the U.K.; www.avis.com). **Budget** (tel. 800/527–0700; 0870/156–5656 in the U.K.; www.budget.com). **Dollar** (tel. 800/800–6000; 0124/622–0111 in the U.K., where it's affiliated with Sixt; 02/9223–1444 in Australia; www.dollar.com). **Hertz** (tel. 800/654–3001; 800/263–0600 in Canada; 020/8897–2072 in the U.K.; 02/9669–2444 in

Australia; 09/256–8690 in New Zealand; www.hertz.com).
National Car Rental (tel. 800/227–7368; 020/8680–4800 in the
U.K.; www.nationalcar.com).

➤ **IN DUBLIN: Avis** (1 Hanover St. E, tel. 01/677–5204; Dublin
Airport, tel. 01/844–5204). **Budget** (151 Lower Drumcondra Rd.,
tel. 01/837–9802; Dublin Airport, tel. 01/844–5919). **Dan Dooley**
(42–43 Westland Row, tel. 01/677–2723; Dublin Airport, tel. 01/
844–5156). **Hertz** (Leeson St. Bridge, tel. 01/660–2255; Dublin
Airport, tel. 01/844–5466). **Murray's Rent-a-Car** (Baggot St.
Bridge, tel. 01/668–1777; Dublin Airport, tel. 01/844–4179).

INSURANCE

When driving a rented car you are generally responsible for any
damage to or loss of the vehicle. Before you rent, see what
coverage your personal auto-insurance policy and credit cards
provide.

Before you buy collision coverage, check your existing
policies—you may already be covered. However, collision
policies that car-rental companies sell for European rentals
usually do not include stolen-vehicle coverage.

REQUIREMENTS & RESTRICTIONS

In Ireland your own driver's license is acceptable. An
International Driver's Permit is a good idea; it's available from
the American or Canadian Automobile Association and, in the
United Kingdom, from the Automobile Association or Royal
Automobile Club. These international permits are universally
recognized, and having one in your wallet may save you a
problem with the local authorities.

Most rental companies require you to be over 23 to rent a car in
Ireland (a few will rent to those over 21) and to have had a license
for more than a year. Some companies also refuse to rent to
visitors over 70.

Car Travel

The number of cars in Ireland has grown exponentially in the last few years, and nowhere has their impact been felt more than in Dublin, where the city's complicated one-way streets are congested during the morning and evening rush hours and often during much of the rest of the day. If you can, avoid driving a car except to get you into and out of the city, and be sure to ask your hotel or guest house for clear directions to get you out of the city.

EMERGENCIES

Membership in a breakdown service is definitely advisable if you're using your own car in Ireland. The Automobile Association of Ireland is a sister organization of its English counterpart and is highly recommended.

➤ **CONTACTS: Automobile Association of Ireland** (tel. 01/617–9999, www.aairland.ie).

GASOLINE

You'll find gas stations along most roads. Self-service is the norm in larger establishments. Major credit cards and traveler's checks are usually accepted. Prices are near the lower end for Europe with a liter of unleaded gas priced around €.90 a liter or about double the gasoline costs in the U.S. Prices tend to vary significantly from station to station, so it is worth driving around the block.

RULES OF THE ROAD

The Irish, like the British, **drive on the left-hand side of the road.** Safety belts must be worn by the driver and front passenger, and children under 12 must travel in the back unless riding in a car seat. It is compulsory for motorcyclists and their passengers to wear helmets.

Drunk-driving laws are strict. The legal limit is 80 milligrams of alcohol per 100 milliliters of blood. Ireland has a Breathalyzer test, which the police can administer anytime. If you refuse to take it, the odds are you'll be prosecuted anyway. As always, the best advice is **don't drink if you plan to drive.**

Parking in Dublin can be a problem. Signs with the letter P indicate that parking is permitted; a stroke through the P warns you to stay away or you'll be liable for a fine of €19.05–€63.50; however, if you get towed, the fine is €190.45. Parking lots are your best bet, but check the rates first; they can vary wildly.

Consumer Protection

Whenever shopping or buying travel services in Ireland, **pay with a major credit card,** if possible, so you can cancel payment or get reimbursed if there's a problem. If you're doing business with a particular company for the first time, **contact your local Better Business Bureau and the attorney general's offices** in your state and (for U.S. businesses) the company's home state as well. Have any complaints been filed? Finally, if you're buying a package or tour, always **consider travel insurance** that includes default coverage (☞ Insurance, *below*).

➤ **BBBS: Council of Better Business Bureaus** (4200 Wilson Blvd., Suite 800, Arlington, VA 22203, tel. 703/276–0100, fax 703/525–8277, www.bbb.org).

Customs & Duties

When shopping, **keep receipts** for all purchases. Upon reentering the country, **be ready to show customs officials what you've bought.** If you feel a duty is incorrect or object to the way your clearance was handled, note the inspector's badge number and ask to see a supervisor. If the problem isn't resolved, write to the appropriate authorities, beginning with the port director at your point of entry.

IN IRELAND

Clearing customs at major gateway airports is a fairly quick and easy procedure. Duty-free allowances have been abolished for those traveling between countries in the European Union (Austria, Belgium, Denmark, Finland, France, Germany, Greece, Ireland, Italy, Luxembourg, the Netherlands, Portugal, Spain [but not the Canary Islands], Sweden, the United Kingdom, but not the Channel Islands or Gibraltar).

For goods purchased outside the EU, you may import duty-free: (1) 200 cigarettes or 100 cigarillos or 50 cigars or 250 grams of smoking tobacco; (2) 2 liters of wine, and either 1 liter of alcoholic drink over 22% volume or 2 liters of alcoholic drink under 22% volume (sparkling or fortified wine included); (3) 50 grams (60 mls) of perfume and ¼ liter of toilet water; and (4) other goods (including beer) to a value of €180.30 per person (€92.70 per person for travelers under 15 years of age).

Goods that cannot be freely imported to the Irish Republic include firearms, ammunition, explosives, illegal drugs, indecent or obscene books and pictures, oral smokeless tobacco products, meat and meat products, poultry and poultry products, plants and plant products (including shrubs, vegetables, fruit, bulbs, and seeds), meat and meat products, and hay or straw even used as packing. Domestic cats and dogs from outside the United Kingdom and live animals from outside Northern Ireland must be quarantined for six months.

➤ **INFORMATION: Customs and Excise** (Irish Life Building, 2nd floor, Middle Abbey St., Dublin 1, tel. 01/878–8811, www.revenue.ie).

IN AUSTRALIA

Australian residents who are 18 or older may bring home $A400 worth of souvenirs and gifts (including jewelry), 250 cigarettes or 250 grams of tobacco, and 1,125 ml of alcohol (including wine, beer, and spirits). Residents under 18 may bring back

$A200 worth of goods. Prohibited items include meat products. Seeds, plants, and fruits need to be declared upon arrival.

➤ **INFORMATION: Australian Customs Service** (Regional Director, Box 8, Sydney, NSW 2001, Australia, tel. 02/9213–2000, fax 02/9213–4000, www.customs.gov.au).

IN CANADA

Canadian residents who have been out of Canada for at least seven days may bring home C$500 worth of goods duty-free. If you've been away fewer than seven days but more than 48 hours, the duty-free allowance drops to C$200; if your trip lasts 24–48 hours, the allowance is C$50. You may not pool allowances with family members. Goods claimed under the C$500 exemption may follow you by mail; those claimed under the lesser exemptions must accompany you. Alcohol and tobacco products may be included in the seven-day and 48-hour exemptions but not in the 24-hour exemption. If you meet the age requirements of the province or territory through which you reenter Canada, you may bring in, duty-free, 1.14 liters (40 imperial ounces) of wine or liquor or 24 12-ounce cans or bottles of beer or ale. If you are 16 or older you may bring in, duty-free, 200 cigarettes and 50 cigars. Check ahead of time with Revenue Canada or the Department of Agriculture for policies regarding meat products, seeds, plants, and fruits.

You may send an unlimited number of gifts worth up to C$60 each duty-free to Canada. Label the package UNSOLICITED GIFT— VALUE UNDER $60. Alcohol and tobacco are excluded.

➤ **INFORMATION: Revenue Canada** (2265 St. Laurent Blvd. S, Ottawa, Ontario K1G 4K3, Canada, tel. 613/993–0534; 800/461–9999 in Canada, fax 613/991–4126, www.ccra-adrc.gc.ca).

IN NEW ZEALAND

Homeward-bound residents 17 or older may bring back $700 worth of souvenirs and gifts. Your duty-free allowance also includes 4.5 liters of wine or beer; one 1,125-ml bottle of spirits; and either 200 cigarettes, 250 grams of tobacco, 50 cigars, or a combination of the three up to 250 grams. Prohibited items include meat products, seeds, plants, and fruits.

➤ **INFORMATION: New Zealand Customs** (Custom House, 50 Anzac Ave., Box 29, Auckland, New Zealand, tel. 09/300–5399, fax 09/359–6730, www.customs.govt.nz).

IN THE U.K.

If you are a U.K. resident and your journey was wholly within the European Union (EU), you won't have to pass through customs when you return to the United Kingdom. If you plan to bring back large quantities of alcohol or tobacco, check EU limits beforehand.

➤ **INFORMATION: HM Customs and Excise** (St. Christopher House, Southwark, London SE1 0TE, U.K., tel. 020/7928–3344, www.hmce.gov.uk).

IN THE U.S.

U.S. residents who have been out of the country for at least 48 hours (and who have not used the $400 allowance or any part of it in the past 30 days) may bring home $400 worth of foreign goods duty-free.

U.S. residents 21 and older may bring back 1 liter of alcohol duty-free. In addition, regardless of your age, you are allowed 200 cigarettes and 100 non-Cuban cigars. Antiques, which the U.S. Customs Service defines as objects more than 100 years old, enter duty-free, as do original works of art done entirely by hand, including paintings, drawings, and sculptures.

You may also mail or ship packages home duty-free: up to $200 worth of goods for personal use, with a limit of one parcel per addressee per day (except alcohol or tobacco products or perfume worth more than $5); label the package PERSONAL USE and attach a list of its contents and their retail value. Do not label the package UNSOLICITED GIFT or your duty-free exemption will drop to $100. Mailed items do not affect your duty-free allowance on your return.

➤ **INFORMATION: U.S. Customs Service** (1300 Pennsylvania Ave. NW, Washington, DC 20229, www.customs.gov; inquiries tel. 202/354–1000; complaints c/o 1300 Pennsylvania Ave. NW, Room 5.4D, Washington, DC 20229; registration of equipment c/o Resource Management, tel. 202/927–0540).

Embassies

Embassies are open weekdays 9–1 and 2–5.

➤ **AUSTRALIA:** (Fitzwilton House, Wilton Terr., tel. 01/676–1517).

➤ **CANADA:** (65 St. Stephen's Green, tel. 01/478–1988).

➤ **SOUTH AFRICA:** (Earlsfort Centre, tel. 01/661–5553).

➤ **UNITED KINGDOM:** (29 Merrion Rd., tel. 01/205–3700).

➤ **UNITED STATES:** (42 Elgin Rd., tel. 01/668–8777).

Emergencies

Dublin's Eastern Help Board can provide the names of doctors. The Dublin Dental Hospital has emergency facilities and lists of dentists offering emergency care. Hamilton Long, a Dublin pharmacy, is open Monday–Wednesday and Saturday 8:30–6, Thursday 8:30–8, and Friday 8:30–7. Temple Bar Pharmacy is open Monday–Wednesday and Friday–Saturday 9–7, Thursday 9–8.

➤ **DOCTORS AND DENTISTS: Dublin Dental Hospital** (20 Lincoln Pl., tel. 01/662–0766). **Eastern Help Board** (tel. 01/679–0700).

➤ **EMERGENCY SERVICES: Gardai (police), ambulance, fire** (tel. 999).

➤ **HOSPITALS: Beaumont** (Beaumont Rd., tel. 01/837–7755).
Mater (Eccles St., tel. 01/830–1122). **St. James's** (1 James St., tel.
01/453–7941). **St. Vincent's** (Elm Park, tel. 01/269–4533).

➤ **LATE-NIGHT PHARMACIES: Hamilton Long** (5 Upper O'Connell
St., tel. 01/874–8456). **Temple Bar Pharmacy** (20 E. Essex St.,
Temple Bar, tel. 01/670–9751).

Holidays

Irish national holidays in 2002 are as follows: January 1; March 17
(St. Patrick's Day; public holiday on Monday, March 18, because
March 17 is a Sunday); March 29 (Good Friday); April 1 (Easter
Monday); May 6 (May Day); June 3 and August 5 (summer bank
holidays); October 28 (autumn bank holiday); and December
25–26 (Christmas and St. Stephen's Day). If you plan to visit at
Easter, remember that theaters and cinemas are closed for the
last three days of the preceding week.

Insurance

The most useful travel-insurance plan is a comprehensive policy
that includes coverage for trip cancellation and interruption,
default, trip delay, and medical expenses (with a waiver for
preexisting conditions).

Without insurance you will lose all or most of your money if you
cancel your trip, regardless of the reason. Default insurance
covers you if your tour operator, airline, or cruise line goes out of
business. Trip-delay covers expenses that arise because of
bad weather or mechanical delays. Study the fine print when
comparing policies.

Always buy travel policies directly from the insurance company;
if you buy them from a cruise line, airline, or tour operator that
goes out of business you probably will not be covered for the
agency or operator's default, a major risk. Before making any

purchase, **review your existing health and home-owner's policies** to find what they cover away from home.

➤ **TRAVEL INSURERS: In the U.S.: Access America** (6600 W. Broad St., Richmond, VA 23230, tel. 804/285–3300 or 800/284–8300, fax 804/673–1586, www.previewtravel.com). **Travel Guard International** (1145 Clark St., Stevens Point, WI 54481, tel. 715/345–0505 or 800/826–1300, fax 800/955–8785, www.travelguard.com).

➤ **INSURANCE INFORMATION: In the U.K.: Association of British Insurers** (51–55 Gresham St., London EC2V 7HQ, U.K., tel. 020/7600–3333, fax 020/7696–8999, www.abi.org.uk). In Canada: **RBC Travel Insurance** (6880 Financial Dr., Mississauga, Ontario L5N 7Y5, Canada, tel. 905/791–8700; 800/668–4342 in Canada, fax 905/816–2498, www.royalank.com). In Australia: **Insurance Council of Australia** (Level 3, 56 Pitt St., Sydney NSW 2000, tel. 03/9614–1077, fax 03/9614–7924). In New Zealand: **Insurance Council of New Zealand** (Level 7, 111–115 Customhouse Quay, Box 474, Wellington, New Zealand, tel. 04/472–5230, fax 04/473–3011, www.icnz.org.nz).

Lodging

The Irish Tourist Board (ITB) has an official grading system and publishes a list of "approved accommodations," which includes hotels, guest houses, bed-and-breakfasts, farmhouses, hostels, and camping parks. For each accommodation, the list gives a maximum charge that no hotel may exceed without special authorization. Prices must be displayed in every room, so if the hotel oversteps its limit, do not hesitate to complain to the hotel manager and/or the ITB. The ITB also distributes five accommodation guides, covering various kinds of lodgings, which are free if obtained in the United States.

The lodgings we list are the cream of the crop in each price category. We always list the facilities that are available—but we don't specify whether they cost extra: when pricing accommodations, always ask what's included and what costs extra. Especially in inexpensive places, some baths may contain a tub and shower, and others may have a shower only. Breakfast will likely be included in the price of your accommodation, except at large hotels. Inquire when booking about bathing facilities and meals if you have specific concerns or needs.

Money Matters

A modest hotel in Dublin costs about €127 a night for two; this figure can be reduced to under €90 by staying in a registered guest house or inn, and reduced to less than €45 by staying in a suburban B&B. Lunch, consisting of a good one-dish plate of bar food at a pub, costs around €7.60; a sandwich at the same pub, about €2.55. In Dublin's better restaurants, dinner will run around €25.40–€38.10 per person, excluding drinks and tip. Theater and entertainment in most places are inexpensive—about €17.80 for a good seat, and double that for a big-name, pop-music concert. For the price of a few drinks and a small entrance fee of about €1.90, you can spend a memorable evening at a *seisun* (pronounced *say-shoon*) in a music pub. Entrance to most public galleries is free, but stately homes and similar attractions normally charge about €3.80 per person. In Dublin, a cup of coffee costs €1.50; pint of beer, €3.50; soda, €1.90; and 2-km (1-mi) taxi ride, €6.

ATMS

ATMs are found in all major towns. Most major banks are connected to CIRRUS or PLUS systems; there is a four-digit maximum for your PIN.

CREDIT CARDS

Throughout this guide, the following abbreviations are used: **AE,** American Express; **DC,** Diners Club; **MC,** MasterCard; and **V,** Visa.

➤ **REPORTING LOST CARDS: American Express** (tel. 0353/1205–5111). **Diners Club** (tel. 0353/661–1800). **MasterCard** (tel. 1800/557378). **Visa** (tel. 1800/558002).

CURRENCY

The Irish Republic is a member of the European Monetary Union (EMU). On January 1, 2002 euro coins and notes will be introduced. From that date all noncash transactions, such as credit cards, will be in euros. The local currency, the pound or punt, will cease to be legal tender by February 9, 2002.

Euro notes come in denominations of €500, €200, €100, €50, €20, €10 and €5. The euro is divided into 100 cents, and coins are available as €2 and €1 and 50, 20, 10, 5, 2, and 1 cents. The euro can be used in 11 other European countries: Austria, Belgium, Finland, France, Germany, Greece, Italy, Luxembourg, the Netherlands, Portugal, and Spain.

CURRENCY EXCHANGE

Dollars and British pounds are accepted only in large hotels and shops geared to tourists. Elsewhere you will be expected to use the euro.

At press time, the euro stood at around U.S.$.85, Canadian $1.30, U.K.£.61, Australian $1.66, and New Zealand $2.10. The punt stood at around €1.27, U.S.$1.10, Canadian $1.65, U.K.£.77, Australian $2.10, and New Zealand $2.60; however, these rates will inevitably change both before and during 2002. Keep a sharp eye on the exchange rate.

For the most favorable rates, **change money through banks.** Although ATM transaction fees may be higher abroad than at home, ATM rates are excellent because they are based on wholesale rates offered only by major banks. You won't do as well at exchange booths in airports or rail and bus stations, in hotels, in restaurants, or in stores. To avoid lines at airport exchange booths, **get a bit of local currency before you leave home.**

➤ **EXCHANGE SERVICES: International Currency Express** (tel. 888/278–6628 for orders, www.foreignmoney.com). **Thomas Cook Currency Services** (tel. 800/287–7362 for telephone orders and retail locations, www.us.thomascook.com).

TRAVELER'S CHECKS

Do you need traveler's checks? It depends on where you're headed. If you're going to rural areas and small towns, go with cash; traveler's checks are best used in cities. Lost or stolen checks can usually be replaced within 24 hours. To ensure a speedy refund, buy your own traveler's checks—don't let someone else pay for them: irregularities like this can cause delays. The person who bought the checks should make the call to request a refund.

Packing

In Ireland you can experience all four seasons in one day, so pack accordingly. Even in July and August, the hottest months of the year, a heavy sweater and a good waterproof coat or umbrella are essential. You should **bring at least two pairs of walking shoes**: it can and does rain at any time of the year, and shoes can get soaked in minutes.

Passports & Visas

When traveling internationally, **carry your passport** even if you don't need one (it's always the best form of ID) and **make two photocopies of the data page** (one for someone at home and another for you, carried separately from your passport). If you lose your passport, promptly call the nearest embassy or consulate and the local police.

ENTERING IRELAND

All U.S., Canadian, Australian, and New Zealand citizens, even infants, need a valid passport to enter Ireland for stays of up to 90 days. Citizens of the United Kingdom, when traveling on flights departing from Great Britain, do not need a passport to enter Ireland.

PASSPORT OFFICES

The best time to apply for a passport or to renew is in fall and winter. Before any trip, check your passport's expiration date, and, if necessary, renew it as soon as possible.

➤ **AUSTRALIAN CITIZENS: Australian Passport Office** (tel. 131–232, www.dfat.gov.au/passports).

➤ **CANADIAN CITIZENS: Canadian Passport Office** (tel. 819/994–3500; 800/567–6868 in Canada, www.dfait-maeci.gc.ca/passport).

➤ **NEW ZEALAND CITIZENS: New Zealand Passport Office** (tel. 04/494–0700, www.passports.govt.nz).

➤ **U.K. CITIZENS: London Passport Office** (tel. 0870/521–0410, www.ukpa.gov.uk) for fees and documentation requirements and to request an emergency passport.

➤ **U.S. CITIZENS: National Passport Information Center** (tel. 900/225–5674; calls are 35¢ per minute for automated service, $1.05 per minute for operator service, www.travel.state.gov/npicinfo.html).

Safety

What crime there is in Dublin is often drug related. Sidestreets off O'Connell Street can be dangerous, especially at night. When you park your car, *do not* leave any valuables inside, even under a raincoat on the backseat or in the trunk; be especially careful parking around the Guinness Brewery and the Old Jameson Distillery.

Senior-Citizen Travel

To qualify for age-related discounts, **mention your senior-citizen status up front** when booking hotel reservations (not when checking out) and before you're seated in restaurants (not when paying the bill). When renting a car, ask about promotional car-rental discounts, which can be cheaper than senior-citizen rates.

➤ **EDUCATIONAL PROGRAMS: Elderhostel** (11 Ave. de Lafayette, Boston, MA 02111-1746, tel. 877/426–8056, fax 877/426–2166, www.elderhostel.org). **Interhostel** (University of New Hampshire, 6 Garrison Ave., Durham, NH 03824, tel. 603/862–1147 or 800/733–9753, fax 603/862–1113, www.learn.unh.edu).

Taxes

VALUE-ADDED TAX

When leaving the Irish Republic, U.S. and Canadian visitors get a refund of the value-added tax (VAT), which currently accounts for a hefty 20% of the purchase price of many goods and 12.5% of those that fall outside the luxury category. Apart from clothing, most items of interest to visitors, right down to ordinary toilet soap, are rated at 20%. Most crafts outlets and department stores operate a system called Cashback, which enables U.S. and Canadian visitors to collect VAT rebates in the currency of their choice at Dublin or Shannon Airport on departure. Otherwise, refunds can be claimed from individual stores after returning home. Forms for the refunds must be picked up at the time of purchase, and the form must be stamped by customs before leaving Ireland (including Northern Ireland). Most major stores deduct VAT at the time of sale if goods are to be shipped overseas; however, there is a shipping charge. VAT is not refundable on accommodation, car rental, meals, or any other form of personal services received on vacation.

Global Refund is a VAT refund service that makes getting your money back hassle-free. The service is available Europe-wide at 130,000l affiliated stores. In participating stores, **ask for the Global Refund refund form** (called a Shopping Cheque). Have it stamped like any customs form by customs officials when you leave the European Union (be ready to show customs officials what you've bought). Then take the form to one of the more than 700 Global Refund counters—conveniently located at every major airport and border crossing—and your money will be refunded on the spot in the form of cash, check, or a refund to your credit-card account (minus a small percentage for processing).

➤ **VAT REFUNDS: Global Refund** (99 Main St., Ste. 307, Nyack, NY 10960, tel. 800/566–9828, fax 845/348–1549, www. globalrefund.com).

Taxis

Official licensed taxis, metered and designated by roof signs, do not cruise. Taxi stands are located beside the central bus station, at train stations, O'Connell Bridge, St. Stephen's Green, College Green, and near major hotels; the Dublin telephone directory has a complete list. The initial charge is €2.30 with an additional charge of about €2.05 a kilometer thereafter. The fare is displayed on a meter (make sure it's on). Alternatively, you may phone a taxi company and ask for a cab to meet you at your hotel, but this may cost up to €2.55 extra. Hackney cabs, which also operate in the city, have neither roof signs nor meters and will sometimes respond to hotels' requests for a cab. Negotiate the fare before your journey begins. Although the taxi fleet in Dublin is large, the cabs are nonstandard and some cars are neither spacious nor in pristine condition. Cab Charge has a reliable track record. Metro is one of the city's biggest but also the busiest. VIP Taxis usually has a car available for a longer trip.

➤ **TAXI COMPANIES: Cab Charge** (tel. 01/677–2222). **Metro** (tel. 01/668–3333). **VIP Taxis** (tel. 01/478–3333).

Telephones

Ireland's telephone system is up to the standards of the United Kingdom and the United States. Direct-dialing is common; local phone numbers have five to eight digits. You can make international calls from most phones, and some cell phones also work here, depending on the carrier.

Do not make calls from your hotel room unless it's absolutely necessary. Practically all hotels add 200% to 300% to the cost of a call.

AREA & COUNTRY CODES

The country code for Ireland is 353, and the area code for Dublin is 01. When dialing an Irish number from abroad, drop the initial 0 from the local area code. The country code is 1 for the United States and Canada, 61 for Australia, 64 for New Zealand, and 44 for the United Kingdom.

DIRECTORY & OPERATOR ASSISTANCE

If the operator has to connect your call, it will cost at least one-third more than direct dial.

INTERNATIONAL CALLS

International dialing codes can be found in all telephone directories. The international prefix from Ireland is 00. For calls to Great Britain, dial 0044 before the exchange code, and drop the initial zero of the local code. For the United States and Canada dial 001, for Australia 0061, and for New Zealand 0064.

LOCAL CALLS

To make a local call just dial the number direct. Public phones take either coins (€.25 for a call) or cards, but not both. At coin phones just pick up the receiver and deposit the money before you dial the number. At card phones pick up the receiver, wait until the display tells you to insert the card, then dial. A three-minute local call costs €.25; a three-minute long-distance call within the Republic costs about €1.

LONG-DISTANCE CALLS

To make a long-distance call, just dial the area code, then the number. If you are dialing Northern Ireland from the Republic, dial 048 or 4428, followed by the new eight-digit number (e.g., for Belfast, dial either 048/90XX–XXXX or 4428/90XX–XXXX).

LONG-DISTANCE SERVICES

AT&T, MCI, and Sprint access codes make calling long distance relatively convenient, but you may find the local access number blocked in many hotel rooms. First ask the hotel operator to connect you. If the hotel operator balks, ask for an international operator, or dial the international operator yourself. One way to improve your odds of getting connected to your long-distance carrier is to travel with more than one company's calling card (a hotel may block Sprint, for example, but not MCI).

➤ **ACCESS CODES: AT&T Direct** (tel. 1800/550000). **MCI WorldPhone** (tel. 1800/551001). **Sprint International Access** (tel. 1800/552001).

PHONE CARDS

"Callcards" are sold in all post offices and at most newsagents. These come in denominations of 10, 20, and 50 units and range in price from about €2.55 for 10 calls to €20.30 for 100 calls. Card phones are now more popular than coin phones.

PUBLIC PHONES

Public pay phones can be found in street booths and in restaurants, hotels, bars, and shops, some of which display a sign saying YOU CAN PHONE FROM HERE. There are currently at least three different models of pay phones in operation; read the instructions or ask for assistance.

Time

Dublin is 5 hours ahead of New York, 8 hours ahead of Los Angeles and Vancouver, 9 hours ahead of Auckland, and 10 hours ahead of Sydney and Melbourne.

Tipping

In some hotels and restaurants a service charge of around 10%—rising to 15% in a few plush spots—is added to the bill. If in doubt, ask whether service is included. In places where it is included, tipping is not necessary unless you have received particularly good service. But if there is no service charge, add a minimum of 10% to the total.

Tip taxi drivers about 10% of the fare displayed by the meter. Hackney cabs, who make the trip for a prearranged sum, do not expect tips. There are few porters and plenty of baggage trolleys at airports, so tipping is usually not an issue; if you use a porter, €.65 is the minimum. Tip hotel porters about €.65 per large suitcase. Hairdressers normally expect about €1.30. You don't tip in pubs, but for waiter service in a bar, a hotel lounge, or a lounge bar, leave about €.65. It is not customary to tip for concierge service.

Train Travel

An electric railway system, the DART (Dublin Area Rapid Transit), connects Dublin with Howth to the north and Bray to the south on a fast, efficient line. There are 25 stations on the route, which is the best means of getting to seaside destinations such as Howth, Blackrock, Dun Laoghaire, Dalkey, Killiney, and Bray. Train services run from Heuston Station to Kildare Town west of Dublin via Celbridge, Sallins, and Newbridge. From Connolly Station you can catch a train to more distant locations like Malahide, Maynooth, Skerries, and Drogheda to the north of Dublin and Wicklow and Arklow to the south.

FARES AND SCHEDULES

DART service starts at 6:30 AM and runs until 11:30 PM; at peak periods, 8–9:30 AM and 5–7 PM, trains arrive every five minutes. At other times of the day, the intervals between trains are 15 to 25 minutes. You should call ahead to check precise departure times, since they do vary, especially on bank holidays. Tickets can be bought at stations, but it's also possible to buy weekly rail tickets, as well as weekly or monthly "rail-and-bus" tickets, from the Irish Rail Travel Centre. Individual fares begin at €.85 and range up to €1.65. There are heavy penalties for traveling the DART without a ticket. For the Railways and DART Lost and Found, contact the Irish Rail Travel Centre.

➤ **TRAIN INFORMATION: Connolly Station** (Amiens St.). **DART** (tel. 01/836–6222). **Heuston Station** (End of Victoria Quay). **Irish Rail Travel Centre** (35 Lower Abbey St., tel. 01/836–6222). **Pearse Station** (Westland Row).

Visitor Information

The main Dublin Tourism center on Suffolk Street is open July–September, Monday–Saturday 8:30–6, Sunday 11–5:30, and October–June, daily 9–6; at Dublin Airport, daily 8 AM–10 PM; and at the Ferryport, Dun Laoghaire, daily 10–9. Bord Fáilte, the Irish Tourist Board, has its own visitor information offices in the entrance hall of its headquarters at Baggot Street Bridge and is open weekdays 9:15–5:15. A suburban tourist office in Tallaght is open March–December, daily 9:30–5. The Temple Bar Information Centre produces the easy-to-use, annually updated *Temple Bar Guide*, which provides complete listings of the area's hundreds of stores, pubs, restaurants, clubs, galleries, and other cultural venues.

➤ **TOURIST INFORMATION: U.K.** (Ireland House, 150 New Bond St., London W1Y 0AQ, tel. 020/7493–3201, fax 020/7493–9065). **U.S.** (345 Park Ave., New York, NY 10154, tel. 212/418–0800 or 800/223–6470, fax 212/371–9052).

➤ **IN DUBLIN: Bord Fáilte** (Baggot St. Bridge, tel. 01/602–4000 or 1850/230330 [within Ireland], fax 01/602–4100, www.ireland.travel.ie). **Dublin Tourism** (Suffolk St., off Grafton St., tel. 01/605–7700 or 1850/230330 [within Ireland], fax 01/605–

7787, www.visitdublin.com). **Temple Bar Information Centre**
(18 Eustace St., tel. 01/671–5717, fax 01/677–2525).

Web Sites

Check out the World Wide Web when planning your trip. You'll
find everything from weather forecasts to virtual tours of famous
cities. Be sure to visit **Fodors.com** (www.fodors.com), a
complete travel-planning site. You can research prices and book
plane tickets, hotel rooms, rental cars, vacation packages, and
more. Other planning tools include a currency converter and
weather reports, and there are loads of links to travel resources.

For a comprehensive directory of sites on Ireland, visit
www.irishabroad.com. Some of the most popular sites (note
that their log-on addresses are subject to change) are as follows:
Best of Ireland (www.iol.ie/~discover/welcome.htm); Every
Celtic Thing on the Web (www.og-man.net); and Heritage
Ireland (www.heritageireland.ie). In addition, many of the
leading newspapers of Ireland have their own Web sites, which
can be gold mines of timely information about special events,
the latest restaurants, and newest cultural happenings. Track
down these newspaper Web sites using a search engine.

When to Go

Summer remains the most popular time to visit Ireland, and for
good reason. The weather is pleasant, the days are long
(daylight lasts until after 10 in late June and July), and the
countryside is green and beautiful. But there will be crowds in
popular holiday spots, and prices for accommodations are at
their peak. Unless you are determined to enjoy the short (July
and August) swimming season, you would be well advised to
take your vacation in Ireland outside peak travel months.

Fall and spring are good times to travel (late September can often
be dry and warm, although the weather can be unpredictable).

Seasonal hotels, restaurants, and accommodations usually close from early or mid-November until mid-March or Easter. During this off-season, prices are considerably lower than in summer, but your selection of hotels and restaurants is limited, and many minor attractions also close. St. Patrick's Week in March gives a focal point to a spring visit, but some American visitors may find the saint's-day celebrations a little less enthusiastic than the ones back home. Dublin, however, welcomes American visitors on March 17 with a weekend-long series of activities, including a parade and the Lord Mayor's Ball. If you're planning an Easter visit, don't forget that most theaters close from Thursday to Sunday of Holy Week (the week preceding Easter), and all bars and restaurants, except those serving hotel residents, close on Good Friday.

If you want to feel like the only tourist in town, **try a winter visit.** Many hotels arrange special Christmas packages with entertainment and outdoor activities; horse races and hunting trips abound. Mid-November to mid-February is either too cold or too wet for all but the keenest golfers, but some of the coastal links courses are playable in almost any weather. There are cheerful open fires in almost all hotels and bars, and, with extra time on their hands, people tend to take an added interest in visitors.

CLIMATE

What follows are average daily maximum and minimum temperatures for Dublin.

➤ **FORECASTS: Weather Channel Connection** (tel. 900/932–8437), 95¢ per minute from a Touch-Tone phone.

CLIMATE CHART

Jan.	47F	8C	May	59F	15C	Sept.	63F	17C
	34	1		43	6		49	9
Feb.	47F	8C	June	65F	18C	Oct.	58F	14C
	36	2		49	9		43	6
Mar.	50F	10C	July	68F	20C	Nov.	50F	10C
	38	3		52	11		40	4
Apr.	56F	13C	Aug.	67F	20C	Dec.	47F	8C
	40	4		52	11		38	3

index

FODOR'S POCKET DUBLIN

EDITORS: Nuha Ansari, Kathy Kattenburg Astor, Lauren A. Myers
Editorial Contributors: Muriel Bolger, Anthony Howard
Editorial Production: Stacey Kulig
Maps: David Lindroth, *cartographer*; Bob Blake and Rebecca Baer, *map editors*
Design: Fabrizio La Rocca, *creative director*; Tigist Getachew, *art director*; Jolie Novak, *senior picture editor*; Melanie Marin, *photo editor*
Production/Manufacturing: Robert B. Shields
Cover Photograph (Merrion Square): Abbie Enock, Travel Ink/Corbis

COPYRIGHT

Fourth Edition

ISBN 0–676–90131–X

ISSN 1098–965X

IMPORTANT TIP

Although all prices, opening times, and other details in this book are based on information supplied to us at press time, changes occur all the time in the travel world, and Fodor's cannot accept responsibility for facts that become outdated or for inadvertent errors or omissions. So **always confirm information when it matters,** especially if you're making a detour to visit a specific place.

SPECIAL SALES